SURRENDERING TO ABUNDANCE

RECEIVING AND GIVING SPIRIT-FILLED MESSAGES

DAVE NEVINS

ABUNDANCE.DAVENEVINS.COM

ISBN: 978-1512049237

INTRODUCTION

I.   MESSAGES

II. INTERVIEW

III. RECEIVING AND GIVING MESSAGES

INTRODUCTION

What you are about to read can seem way off the grid. I can sympathize with that. But since there is such huge potential upside to this subject matter, please give me a few paragraphs to present the goods.

This is a collection of profoundly encouraging writings on the most astonishing topic—which is of course, God. Since this subject sometimes seems too inaccessible, we'll explore practical, personal, intriguing ways we can genuinely encounter more of God's love, in spite of anything attempting to prevent it.

The material comes from what I call "classical-progressive" Christian treasures. That is, not much is new, yet it is likely unfamiliar.

The focal point here is one particularly striking gift offered us: the capacity to hear God's direct guidance—believe it or not. The messages can arrive in first-person, word-for-word, as did the many within this book. This may sound too incredible to be legit, but it's actually a more common occurrence today than we might think, which we'll see below, as we unwrap the gift.

In fact, Jesus made it clear years ago he would speak to us today, unpacking what he said before. [John 14:26]

I'm Dave Nevins, an informal leader in various Washington D.C. environments that help activate this "two-way" prayer.

The inspiring examples in *Surrendering to Abundance* were received from a long-time friend of mine. Though he doesn't mind using his full name, we've decided to omit it, only to avoid excess social media. You can read about his story in the Section II Interview, and about mine in Section III, Receiving and Giving Messages.

Of course we're not experts, but thankfully that's not a requirement. Anyone can simply receive.

How This Book is Different

There are similar, excellent books on the market, for example:

- Sarah Young's extremely popular *Jesus Calling*;
- Hal Helm's terrific *Echoes of Eternity*;
- F. J. Robert's classic *Come Away My Beloved*.

But we wanted this book to be a bit different.

Reading the other publications is like listening in on someone else's phone, but this one also tries to boost the bandwidth on your own device, perhaps a little more broadly.

So if you're interested in an increased explicit connection, this can be a great resource. Use what you want.

Table of Contents

To that end, we provide three approaches:

I. Section One contains over 150 messages.

II. Section Two has an interview with the message recipient, my friend, who shares his story of how his gift was cultivated, including valuable support to unpack God's extraordinary presents, often lying dormant within us.

III. Section Three presents lessons learned and frequently asked questions such as:

- What are we to make of this?
- How do you discern?
- Could it be just the imagination?
- What does it sound and feel like?
- Can anybody have the gift?
- What are tips to opening up?
- How does it fit into God's larger story plot?

Tips for Reading the Messages

Before starting, here are a few key points prior to reading further. (These common issues are expanded in Section Three, Receiving and Giving Messages).

1. The writings are not attempted additions to the Bible, but rather sample fulfillments of how Jesus said the Spirit would lead us. For example, if the Bible were a DVD, then the Spirit shines the laser illuminating a precise part, right on time. In other words, modern prophecy does not add chapters to the disc, but simply highlights what to watch.

2. It's easy to presume these messages have a power over us solely because they are worded in first-person. But they don't. Every person is an artistic, unique, unrepeatable effect of God's love and no one's connection has the primary authority over another. At the center of the heart is a private encrypted line between each person and God.

3. These words were given to a particular person, with a particular personality type, in a particular season. Therefore some parts will apply to us and other parts won't. We need to read these, as we would treat anything in life, listening for what the Spirit desires to accent and encourage for us at the time. God's revelations for us are personalized.

With that in mind, there is a magnificent storehouse of wealth here. Enjoy!

SECTION ONE: MESSAGES

ENTER INTO MY PRESENCE

The Lord God is so much more than your songs, prayers, visions, thoughts—anything you can attempt to conceive of Me falls universes short of the least of My power.

I transcend the earthly realm so greatly, so magnificently. If you only believed, for faith is truly the only vehicle I can give to My people to tap into My awesome being. There is no other faculty you possess that can begin to touch this.

Intellect, imagination, deep thoughts are earthly gifts I give you, but they bring you no closer to My victory. This is why My graces are as open to the learned as to the uneducated, even to those lame of mind.

The spirit in a man overcomes all for it is his connection to the eternal. Begin to tap into it more. Books and treatises are only helpful to the extent they might light a spark, but it is only your divine communion to the Savior that brings life-changing power.

"I am the Alpha and Omega." My infinite grace, power, knowledge, resources encompassed by My passionate love for you enter into every situation where you call on Me to intercede.

Do not believe the lies—anything that ever causes you to think any less of My greatness and what I am capable of completely metamorphosizing—is a lie.

I am more awesome in all I am than you will ever conceive in a million lifetimes.

Mankind still fails to define or describe Me after how many centuries?

Don't think too long on Me—just enter into My presence and I will do the rest.

> *She sat at the Lord's feet, listening to what he said.*
> *Luke 10:38-41*

An Ever-Living, Present God

Never let Me become just words, a ritual, a philosophy or anything you merely perform to try to bring about My grace. I am an ever-living, present God, longing to commune directly with you. I am not a religion. I am so much more if only you seek My face with a sincere and pure heart.

I need more than your periodic attention to a prayer time or a book of words. I am alive and living in this world.

Do you know how much I long to burst through to the world with the power of My presence, My life-changing love? Words, visions, and prophecy are only symbols pointing My way. Words cannot describe Me, feelings cannot contain Me—I am existing in realms of glory you don't yet know, filling places within your faithfulness and My leadings.

Never, never underestimate Me and how I envelop you and your situations. Your mind can't begin to comprehend it, where I'm coming from, where I'll go in your situation, the grace I'll bestow, the glorious renewal I always bring. There is no hopelessness in Me.

I will always intervene when you invite Me in—and even when you do not. I love you too much to leave the situation the same. There is too much of My presence available to settle.

Keep seeking, keep asking, keep receiving. Be open and get ready for all of Me. I won't hold back—I don't have to—My portion is infinitely full and more than you'll need. Expect it all from Me and I'll take you beyond.

> *My soul thirsts for God, for the living God.*
> *Psalm 42:2*

ALL IN ALL

You come seeking My insight, yet I say to you I am your all in all—I am already in all you do and say. You never have to look for My direction and grace for didn't I promise I would never leave you or forsake you? Do not increase your fretting trying to find Me or seek additional directions. I know what you need when you need it, and exactly what you need it for.

I would long that you merely seek the rest of coming into and being in My presence. It is there we can commune—where you will find peace, joy, wisdom, healing, direction—anything of the abundance of My flow in your life.

Often it is when you strive to hear from Me that you will miss out on what I want to say. I always long to connect at the inner depths and it is a challenge for you to hear Me when you exert the control and are not a surrendered vessel, open to My truth, My light.

Do what it takes in the natural for you to find peace for I am never too far from My created world that you cannot find Me there. Sometimes a walk, or a drive or some other less concentrated act can bring you to the door of our communing. Go there if need be. For every prayer time is simply the time where I desire to connect to you intimately, My beloved.

I always want our times together to go both ways for though you have much to say to Me, I have so much more I long to impart in you to bring you deeply to the place of being like Jesus, to share in this awesome love of the Trinity that knows no limit.

I have a waterfall of love for you, of the riches of My grace—every time we commune—which is all the time, but, in our more intimate times together in prayer, praise and worship.

I want you to know it, to sense it, to feel it, experience it—to know the love of God which surpasses all human understanding. Then, you will know I am a real and present God, alive and well and as close as your heart.

Others will see this in you and will desire what you are. Share with them your good news and let us work together to share the Kingdom of My love.

...so that God may be all in all.
I Corinthians 15:28

My Generous Hand

The beginning of faith is surrender. Be amazed at how much I do when you let go.

Begin to trust Me deeply, in the depths of your heart. As your faith is rich, you will know the freedom of surrendering to Me, not the angst of trying to hold on to something for which you have no control.

Faith involves knowing My face so lovingly, My heart so dearly, that you know in your own heart that My generous hand will provide.

I am your God. It is in My nature to lavish My people with what they need and more. As you begin to truly trust Me, you'll know that this lavish provision takes many forms—many unknown, most unexpected, but always exactly meeting your needs when you need them met.

Go deeper with Me—in prayer, in fellowship, in scripture reading, in just being with Me.

I want you to know My heart, know Me, for it is there you'll begin to experience Me in My love and where you'll know My heavenly provision for your earthly needs.

Fear not, little flock,
for it is your Father's good pleasure
to give you the Kingdom.
Luke 12:32

SEEK MY REST

I long to minister to My saints for it is only when you are filled by Me that you are at all ready to face the daily battle set before you. My ministering equips you with peace, strength, endurance, and the will to carry on in circumstances where you would otherwise fall. Know that My Spirit must go before you in any area that I have called you to be My agent. Seek My rest, let go and allow Me to have My way in you.

You, as saints, are worthy vessels created to carry out My work on earth. Never doubt My power in you. Remember, you are merely the agent, the venue of a great work begun in Heaven to carry and release into My created world. Understand you can do anything I call you to, for it is not a matter of being able as it is your desire to serve My purposes. When you're willing, I am always ready and able.

Come away and spend time with Me, hear My voice, see what it is I am calling you to. "Understand what the will of the Lord is." Let Me heal you and strengthen you so you can be with Me, so you can hear the sound of My voice that will guide you into battle.

Let Me minister to you—I will bring you what you need to heed My call, be it healing, sustenance, or the peace of mind to trust Me. Out of our being one will come your doing, a doing that will shine My light and fulfill what I intend for it to accomplish.

Come with Me to a quiet place and get some rest.
Mark 10:45

You and Me

Life is not about waiting for and collecting blessings. If you look only for the blessing, you will miss Me as I pass on by once you collect your goods.

This life is first and foremost about your relationship with Me. Does anyone still know that a life of blessedness flows from our relating? The true blessings of life are attained in your knowing Me, for there is no higher attainment. Everything else you'll ever gain—wealth, health, prestige—all of it will be gone one day.

Look for Me in these and other possessions for I augment each part of life and put the proper touch into it in such a way that you'll know where things belong and how fleeting possessions of any kind are.

I bring seasons of anointing to areas of your life that only last for a time—some as short as a sunset, others as long as another's life. But in the end, it all comes back to you and Me.

It is in this connection that true love finds its expression, a love that builds My Kingdom on the earth and prepares the way for your coming to Me, closer and closer with each step, together forever, a love unmatched in the universe.

Let us love as I have ordained it. Do not let My gifts for you ever be a source of entanglement. For the true light that shines brightest, shines when you come to Me with open hearts and hands, yearning only to know and love Me more deeply.

*A man's life does not consist
in the abundance of his possessions.
Luke 12:15*

See the World Through Me

You'll never find the full satisfaction in anything in this world, nor should you seek it there. It is only in Me. Your job, relationships, living space are all secondary to the glory you'll find in Me. Don't go looking for comfort and peace in these things.

You must come to know Me into a new dimension, one that sees the world's things through Me first. You seek comfort in many areas: the past, the present, the future, family, friends—it's all about Me, My grace, My supply, My love.

Life does not consist in the abundance of anything you have here. It's all Me. Seek My face.

There's always another condition you seek to attach to earthly things to seek their "perfection"—one more trait, whether it's your job, a mate, family, living arrangement. Do you suppose you know perfection? Your sense of it is based on earthly influence—past hurts, lust, fear, a desire for personally fashioned comfort. You do not know what grace can do when you attach conditions to it.

Why can't you trust My overflow? Believe and receive.

It is God who arms me with strength
and makes my way perfect.
II Samuel 22:33

LIFE WORSHIP

I am not a part of your life; I am your life. There is nothing that should stand before Me: worries, fears, relationships, goals, career. I am your all-consuming God.

Live for Me. Do not detach your spirit from your soul. Worship Me. There is a simpler life in life worship. I don't just get magnified in praise time.

If you live it you'll see the manifestations in all you do. You'll bring My presence to the situation and it will be different. I will be in the midst because of your obedience to praise Me there and then.

Do not let the things of life I've placed and entrusted to you ever become hindrances to Me. All things lead back to Me.

Your perspective is clouding Me out. It's Me first. See all things through Me, then look at life. That's how you'll see what's important.

*You give life to everything,
and the multitudes of Heaven worship you.
Nehemiah 9:6*

FREE FOR MORE ABUNDANCE

Don't let your habits squeeze you from grace. They are virtually invisible ways of the devil staying in. Keep as clear and clean as you can and grace will do the rest.

There is mercy and forgiveness in My love. I am always ready to start again with you. Do not let condemnation get to you in this particular conviction.

You are rebuked to be loved more, to be free for more abundance. It flows through a pure heart. Purify your heart, be diligent to be honest with yourself and you will be surprised how much naturally will flow your way.

This "rod" corrects and protects.

> *He will strike the earth with the rod of his mouth;*
> *with the breath of his lips he will slay the wicked.*
> *Isaiah 11:4.*

Follow Me

Do not be lazy and avoid the work of spiritual discipline. Without it, you will not receive all that I have for you.

I am here, waiting to give more. Where are you? Will you follow Me through this maze of life for which I have the map? How could you ever know the way? Each step is carefully sculpted with a detail you could not know, nor could I explain.

I say trust Me because I would only confuse you and cause you greater strain.

Know that I am the God of all. I live in you and therefore I know where I am going, though you don't. I do nothing without a reason. Nothing! Like My Word, I do not waste time, effort, energy. Your life here is too short for that. Believe in Me, for I am your provider.

Walk along side with Me. I am here, with you, loving you, serving you, being in you. I cannot do more right now than I'm already doing. You've got all of Me now—please do not doubt Me or despair, My child.

Love moves Me, faith sustains you. Live for Me. Live for Me. I'm taking care of it all.

*Since we live by the Spirit,
let us keep in step with the Spirit.
Galatians 5:25*

THE WISDOM OF PRAISE

I ask of you your whole spirit, soul, and body, yet so often I get what's in your mind. Do you think too much about your prayer? I'm looking for your heart more than your head.

At times, your thinking can be an enemy to the spirit that I have ingrained in you. Though I have created all of you, it is the balance of all I made you to be that brings out one area to its greatest fulfillment. Unlike exercising a muscle repeatedly where it gets stronger with extended use, exertion of your mind in prayer will concentrate too much power to your known faculties and may cause less reliance on what your spirit is saying. Lead in with your spirit. Experience the wisdom of praise.

I can reach your depths when you enter in to My presence in holy surrender. Your depths of your spirit know far more in time of praise than hours of pondering and questioning. Your most profound insight is most often the product, or byproduct, of the deepest times of prayer.

Once your mind grasps what the spirit is telling it, now you have true direction. It never works in reverse—mind first speaking to spirit. The mind is too finite to probe the deeper things of God. So again I say, lead in with your spirit and connect with My Holy Spirit. I will show you truth.

For the Spirit searches all things, even the deep things of God.
I Corinthians 2:10

My Presence is Joy

I can only give you more when you take hold of less. I have abundance from My throne that only those who love Me from their heart can know.

Mine is a Kingdom of light and I shine where I am free to be steward, to call the shots and nothing short of total surrender will do. God is and always will be your source of hope. Don't pretend that this earth is capable of offering or providing a substitute. The earthly things only offer a reflection of Me for I created it all and am the source. How could anything created hold any real hope? Why cling to it?

You have no reason not to be joyful for My presence is Joy. I have conquered it all; I have won the victory; I know how the game ends and we have won. I call the shots in this life from Heaven.

Remember all I do is infused with My joy and there is no cause ever for despair. Despair is so foreign to My Kingdom; it is strictly the creation of man out of communion with the King of Kings. It does not exist in Heaven, your true Christian home. In essence, it is not real, only real to the extent that you include it in your realm.

Do you not exist in the Heavenly way when all is said and done? Keep ever focused on Me and you, too, will never know desperation.

The joy of the Lord is your strength.
Nehemiah 8:10

LET GO

You do not have to do anything learned. Just listen for My prompting.

Do it and trust. Let go. There is no such thing as control. And there is no real comfort in it.

The true comfort is in abandoning control and abiding in Me. You're off the hook then because you don't have to be responsible for your own willed creations.

You have less rest because you have got your way time and again. Look around and see what it has wrought. Where is the fruit? Fear, lack of joy and peace, striving, "stuckness," disgruntled-ness. Can you look and see good things of your own doing leading anywhere hopeful? This is not Burger King ("Have it your way").

It is My way or no way good. The very things you fear to surrender are the places most full of new grace and possibility. Stop taking things into your own hands. Give it up. You stand to lose nothing but a rather imperfect way of life.

In the same way you have submitted to your fears (causing you to judge, hold back, withdraw, get suspicious, doubt, stand still, be moody, etc.), now you will submit to My promises?—My Word, and a newer and healthier fruit will spring forth (patience, kindness, confidence, peace and inner rest, trusting relationship with Me, moving forward in life, increased faith) and with it an ability to pray more boldly.

And most of all: freedom—to enjoy life, your work, friendships, family, the present with God for who he is, and not what he can do to help your currently meager lifestyle.

It will bring hope, peace, joy, and it will spread the gospel, for it will be contagious. You will see the prosperous life I have called you to, not what you engender to create.

All this by letting go—will you trust Me?

> *Do not fear; just believe.*
> *Mark 5:36*

FLOW IN MY PEACE

You seek as if you might know My ways. Remember, My ways are not your ways. They're better, much better, regardless of how they look. Go with the flow of My peace.

Let Me be God. Show Me no ill will towards My ways. I have love for you and seek your best, more so than you're able to.

Come into My presence with a grateful heart, not murmuring, releasing yourself to free yourself to Me.

You must be free to come to Me, to be ready and able to flow through Me. No personal expectations, but Me. Stop fighting, resisting.

Flow to the point of peace and stop there for your next command. I will show you the way.

Your heart must remain open.
The Lord is near.
Do not be anxious about anything,
but in everything, by prayer and petition,
with thanksgiving, present your requests to God.
And the peace of God, which transcends all understanding,
will guard your hearts and your minds in Christ Jesus.
Philippians 4:5-7

I Will Let You Know

You are in My will and I let you know the times you resist.

So much struggle is spent on second-guessing, causing tension, fear and doubt. It's you and your struggle. I bring joy and peace. You know if you are obeying for My Holy Spirit tells you.

How long can you stay out of My will without Me doing something to guide you?

Life has enough troubles without you adding personal struggle and strife. It's a trust issue.

You have seen how I open amazing doors without your help. I Am.

*For I created all things
and by My will they exist
and have their being.
Revelation 4:11*

BEYOND TO GLORY

I have purposes here and now beyond any bitterness. You look only to your present circumstance. I see beyond, into the eternal.

That is where I am, not in passing things. I am on your side, working in you a greater thing, for your and My glory.

I am still in charge. Let go of pettiness and know that I am above that. You are mine. I have called you by name.

> *Beyond all question, the mystery of Godliness is great:*
> *He appeared in a body,*
> *was vindicated by the Spirit,*
> *was seen by angels,*
> *was preached among the nations,*
> *was believed on in the world,*
> *was taken up in glory.*
> *I Timothy 3:16*

DIVINE CAPACITY

I know your hurts and disappointments, but don't let Me not love you.

I want you to love My people who are as hurt, if not more, than you. Let Me give you the heart to love them.

Your work often reminds you of your pains. It's good learning—you have to be able to love everyone and beware the expectations you place. They're not realistic. You are learning from Me, much more important than what the world teaches. You don't need a credential to validate you and My work for you has nothing to do with that.

Live for Me, but please don't ignore Me or run from Me. You need Me now.

Come for your healing—submit to My love and you can live for others without hurts and you'll have divine capacity to do great things on a small scale.

Despise not the day of small beginnings.
Zechariah 4:10

I Wash Away the Barriers

My cleansing sets you free.

I long to clean away the barriers that this life can cause between us, between what I have for you.

Most are broken by your repentance to Me, where I wash you fully of your sin.

Others are attacks of the enemy, curses, legal rights of the devil that involve more revelation of the Spirit before you are even aware of what is upon you.

I can do spiritual surgery and bring to surface things hitherto unknown, deeper sin, that once revealed, you can let go of in repentance.

> *Wash away all my iniquity*
> *and cleanse me from my sin.*
> *Psalm 51:2*

FREE INDEED

Repentance is not merely the door to a clear conscience to rid you of guilt so you can feel worthy to be in My presence. No, repentance and forgiveness are My gifts to you to help maintain our relationship. For without true repentance, we cannot have a Spirit-led relationship. Repentance is not about feeling good again for you may not afterwards.

But know this in faith—you are My children and I will forgive anything from which your heart seeks a true repentance, with the deepest desire to clear the pathway to Me. Remember—you serve a completely sinless and pure Lord. Without a pure heart, I cannot be free to declare My favor in your life.

Let your deepest desires be to yearn to be free of sin, to let it go, leave it behind, and run to Me. "Whom the Son sets free is free indeed." Do not go back on your sin once repented. Condemnation will destroy you for though you are covered by My blood sacrifice, you will forsake this gift and believe a lie. My Word on forgiveness was made final at the cross and this is the truth you must build your broken life upon. I have set you free to be as Jesus is.

This, My dear ones, is a miracle: sinful man in unison with a glorified God. Together only can we stand in righteousness where you can let Me take your bond of sin and know the power of redemption.

If the Son sets you free, you will be free indeed.
John 8:36

I Defend You

You might have to take a stand for righteousness—in your workplace, in your relationships. Doing this outside of weakness creates self-righteousness, just another sign of your weak defense system.

I will guide you in this light (and yes, it is light). Get used to it, to submissiveness. In it My strength will carry you, and emanate forth from you. No longer will you take My support and use it to fuel your balsawood fortress. You don't like this idea, but yielding (going with the flow) will bring you the much sought after peace you need in this season of life.

Do you really know what it is to rely on Me? Through this, I will show you. Don't think the flesh will engage or embrace it. It won't. But if flesh will die away in this area and you will contend with it no more, you will find freedom in the flow of My love and this love isn't what you're used to—actually it's not what you think love is.

This is part of the chastening that leads to deepening of our love. Embrace it for in it is peace. Others will see it and you will share these words to a restless people.

Turn each time from your anxiety and call on Me. I'm there ready with the next direction for you. Just yield.

I'll show you My way. Give in and give up. You know when your ways are clearly not working.

You want My fruit. You desire truth. I will give it, but only on My path. It is not well trod, but its way is life, light, wisdom and hope.

Peace to all who enter.

> *Trust him and he shall bring it to pass.*
> *Psalm 37:5*

Smokescreens

Go beyond the attacks of the enemy, for they are mere smoke screens to My abundant, anointed flow. The devil's power is only fueled by your doubts, how much you choose to believe the mirage of a lie he puts before you.

So much of the battle between the Kingdom of Good and evil takes place in the mind. But it is there where it stands its only chance for victory as the devil is a defeated foe. Giving the devil place in your thoughts leads you only to lies and destruction.

So often you marvel at My grace and deliverance because you have already been expecting the worst. Only then do you know the joy of believing, but I tell you that you can have joy and peace now if you believe the words of My truth.

Why wait and be crushed under the oppressive weight of anxiety and fear? When you begin to know and believe who I AM, you will know that you are only in the world and not of it.

Therefore, as citizens of Heaven, heirs to the throne, people of a faithful inheritance, covenant people—you are entitled to glory.

We are not unaware of the enemy s schemes.
II Corinthians 2:11

THE VICTOR

You are an overcomer.

My Word is still true despite what you see. Satan fears the goodness and greatness of the Lord in you.

Your fear is nothing to his for he truly has something to fear: the God of the universe against him. The best he can do is to try to make you as miserable as he is. Misery loves company.

> *The Lord your God is the one who goes with you*
> *to fight for you against your enemies to give you victory.*
> *Deuteronomy 20:4*

I RULE

The Lord your God rules over all with power, love, and infinite wisdom. Fear can have no place in the realm of My glory.

So much of your life is physically out of your control, so why don't you accept the fact that I am completely in control?

Come into My presence with thanksgiving and joy. Abound in Me, your everlasting hope. Seek My face and declare My righteousness in your life.

> *Let him who boasts boast about this:*
> *that he understands and knows Me.*
> *Jeremiah 9:24*

Crystal Clear Love

Raise the standard again. Set the Lord before you, not your own deviation of what you've seen.

See the purity of the Lamb. The standard never changes, only you do.

Get back to your first love and you will hear My voice again.

It will be so crystal clear. You will have no doubt. Cleanse the pollution from your mind. It is better to live for Me than to entertain fears, lusts, prejudices.

You are an overcomer because of Me.

Be free and know what it is to have joy unspeakable.

Then the angel showed me the river of the water of life, as clear as crystal, flowing from the throne of God and of the Lamb.
Revelation 22:1

MY PERFECTION IN YOU

Seek not to take control, for that is My job.

It is only yours to carry out what I send you to do, not in your own power, for you are indeed powerless to carry out My tasks.

I need full surrender so I can make your life an offering to others. Let Me work in you.

Give Me just the smallest part of you and I can use that for I know where to go in you and make you a workable vessel for this Kingdom.

Don't think you need perfection for it is My perfection, My strength, My ability that can only work through a surrendered vessel.

It is the Father, living in me, who is doing his work.
John 14:10

SUBSTANTIAL PAYOFF

Deuteronomy 4:29: "But from there you will seek the Lord your God, and you will find him if you seek him with all your heart and with all your soul."

Stay pure within—this is the path to truth and light. Evil does not go where goodness lies and vice versa. Remember this: step from the land of just enough where only mercy carries you—flow into the land set aside for abundant life. It will cost you your flesh, but I say each surrender of self will more than be returned with My overflow, for now is the time to seek My reward.

Stay close by Me and do not let the world mold you, but be transformed. Do not let freedom be your downfall. I have made you free to be free, not to re-enslave yourself. Come out from the midst of them. Let go.

Fall into your faith with deeper abandon. This will require added discipline, but much of that is merely reclaiming what you have let go—in all areas: prayertime, working, eating, exercising, living for others, giving.

Do these with a zeal for the prize—that there is good to be had when we work in unity—Me and you!

I urge you in view of God's mercy,
to offer your bodies as living sacrifices,
holy and pleasing to God—this is your spiritual act of worship.
Romans 12:1

CELLARS OF NEW WINE

Less of Me equals more of you. The way to more is less. Take your cross. Embrace it. Live it. Love it. Know it leads to a greater way of My presence in your life.

Your God longs to be all in your life.

He needs more room to build and grow you. Get out of the way. Do not feed the old ways and let him appear to you.

Abandon fear. Trust more to let him in and you shall see the "glory of the Lord in the land of the living." It is a highway to Heaven, a contentious road, but it brings life to those who tread upon it.

In cleaning the house you must get rid of stuff to let in the new. Get rid of the old wine and wineskins, old relationships, attitudes, finances, job attitudes and methods. I will not take the old into your new. It is dead and death has no place with life.

Come apart for a while and I will consume you in My rest, My blessings of life, more abundantly.

No one pours new wine into old wineskins.
If he does, the wine will burst the skins,
and both the wine and the wineskins will be ruined.
No, he pours new wine into new wineskins.
Mark 2:22.

GOD OF MIRACLES

Why are there so few miracles in the midst of the Body?

I am a God of miracles, one who can bring change instantaneously to a situation, bringing with it a manifestation of power that levels the ground like a mighty storm.

I AM.

I am the God of awesome reality, the God who encompasses all of this universe, all resources; but they pale compared to the limitless resources this side of eternity. And I can bring all that to bear on the Body.

Do you not believe in My awesome power? Why do you hold back? There is nothing difficult for Me. I am wisdom. I am light. The minute My light shines forth, all things are made new.

And this I make available to you today, right now.

Do not squander this anointed gift for it will show the world that Jesus Christ is a living God and he still walks among his people, showing love, life, hope, peace, renewal, and strength.

Live as if you meant it.

> *The miracles I do in my Father's name speak for me.*
> *John 10:25*

REJOICE

Today is a glorious day for My people. Rejoice. I am alive and live and reign in your lives.

The Lord longs for you to carry out his plan today.

There is no waiting, not when you have the power and glory of God at your behest.

Let it unfold into your life and pour out into the world. Today. What are you waiting for? Is there a better time than the present to step out and step up?

What do you lack? Ask for that which you need. Do you want to do My work? Know what you ask—it is a big responsibility only you can carry out as purposed by Me from the beginning of time eternal.

I long to live in My people as I have purposed, not according to your plan or convenience. Break out from your earthly constraint.

Let Me have My way in you and see the glory of God.

*This is the day the Lord has made;
let us rejoice and be glad in it.
Psalm 118:24*

KINGDOM LIVING

Throw off oppression for I live in you, and in Me you live and move and have your being. All that life touches is also touched by Me.

My anointing precedes you, it follows you, it touches everything you do whether you know it or not.

You are instruments in the hands of the Almighty, created for righteous works.

Your limitations do not set Me back. For you were created to do a work for Me and surely your limits do not thwart the plans of God.

Are you a surrendered vessel? Do you seek My will? Do you pray for the Spirit's direction in your life? Are you sincere? Do you put others before yourself? Do you long to do My work above all other? If so, you are prepared for Kingdom living.

I will take you to the point of nothingness in this world and then I will take you beyond the ephemeral, beyond what worldly glories deem great. For there is no great thing outside of My creating it. Let Me in, let Me have My way. For it is your will I seek, to release Me into the awesomeness of this life, as I have planned it.

My favor rests on My people.

Surely the Lord is in this place,
and I was not aware of it.
Genesis 28:16

BEYOND EXPERIENCE

You are an instrument in the hands of a mighty, mighty God.

Do not think your activity is beyond the leading of the Spirit, for a tool only is effective in the hands of the craftsman. I have created you for the Godly purposes to be used in conjunction of the whole of My Body. Like notes in a symphony, each plays a part individually, but finds greater purpose in the whole creation. Do not look to your individual place, how you will use My way independent of a larger plan.

I do not look like society. There are no spiritual entrepreneurs, only humble servants and willing hearts, always looking to the Master for their next command. Work in sync with Me. Life loses its meaning outside of the construct of how I designed.

I know this is often difficult for you, My children, to comprehend in your limited experiential world. I go beyond experience. Do I not raise up fools in the world's eyes to do My work? What earthly things carry weight for My tasks? In the past I've called shepherds, fishermen, thieves, prisoners—unlearned in the world's ways. What, in their human poverty, could they have offered Me? Do not focus on getting ready to do, just be ready to become.

*The Lord does not look at the things man looks at.
Man looks at the outward appearance,
but the Lord looks at the heart.
I Samuel 16:7*

THE ULTIMATE OWNER

You own nothing. And when you die, you'll own less. It is all mine to begin with as well as end with.

So why do you fear controlling that which is not yours? Do you fear control of the rivers, the sky, buildings—anything else that's a part of your life of which you have little or no control? Then why do you assign random control of other things?

I entrust to you a given amount of things, people, events in your lifetime to which you are called to be the steward. Since I am the ultimate owner, you can only work in conjunction with Me to handle them successfully and well. Once you depart from this ownership relation, things can go terribly amiss. And you will lose much; your peace, your vision, your witness, your hope, your success, essentially, your ability to be clay in the hands of the potter.

Do not let fear draw you in to your own world, away from Me. That is a lonesome place, one that exacerbates all your doubts, fears, and worries. "The Lord is your light and your salvation—whom do you fear?"

Bring Me in where you fall short. At the point where you begin to feel out of control, call on Me for it is here I have designed to do My part, where you will witness My power, My intervention, My answer.

You will see, feel, touch, and know the difference.

The one who fears is not made perfect in love.
I John 4:18

LEAP!

I need your whole heart.

Hold back nothing and even more so, do not let anything hinder its release to Me. There are so many locks on your heart: pride, guilt, doubt, self-righteousness, fear, worry, among others. Let go and fall back on Me for once.

Trust that as you leap to Me, I will catch you, as I supported Peter on the water. Nothing of this world supports or encourages leaping. But My Word calls for it and there is no greater truth on which you can rely.

What are you afraid might happen? Have I called you to do it? Then what could go wrong? My Holy Spirit is with you every step of the way of your life anyhow. So why not leap as he directs?

More peace awaits following you stepping out than if you stayed in the boat, where you are left to ponder and imagine in your mind only things that fall far short of the glory I have yet to reveal from one step of faith.

Jesus immediately said to them:
"Take courage! It is I. Don't be afraid."
Matthew 14:27

STEP UP

What are you waiting for? Does revelation always come in the form of a mailed envelope? Will you trust Me to carry out awesome works in you?

"Are you willing?" is more the question than "are you ready?" I have made you ready, an available vessel, ready to conduit grace, to stand and see the glory of the Lord. But I cannot surpass your will. What do you want? What else is there to be done?

Strive no more, My child, and leave the past behind you. Step up and step in to a new place for your life. Let Me lead you, but I need deeper surrender.

Cast away all fear and doubt. Step in and obey. Take the step. Learn from Me. I am your guide. Let trust speak to you for it is the only voice that can clearly penetrate fear and confusion.

Remember, it is Me, the Lord, that guides you in all your ways. This way is no different.

Do not look around you, but look into My eyes and see that I have a wonderful way set up, graced by My anointing.

Just step into it today.

A man's steps are directed by the Lord.
Proverbs 20:24

I Have Your Spirit

You have heard it said, "The flesh is a good servant, but a terrible master." The flesh hinders you from reaching inner depths, from seeing My insights, and it holds you back from the joyful life known by My peace. Do not let it rule in any area of your life. You must resist it for it is a foremost tool for the devil, an avenue into your world.

I want to lead you into a place of holiness where you are sold out for My purposes so that I can begin to use you more in the work of My Kingdom. Always go the way of Jesus—die as he did and do not seek to serve your fleshly carnal ways. I have your spirit and it is enough to show you the way if you submit to it.

Move in faith toward My leading. Your flesh is too fault-filled to be a reliable lead into any endeavor. Don't lead with it; too often it will only deceive you. Die to self continually—the "pain" you feel is your prideful worldly identity falling away. In Me you truly are a new creation. Let Me be your lead for I will help you in this each step of the way. You can do nothing on your own, including the very thing I'm asking you to do: to die to the flesh.

So seek My counsel and begin to rely completely on My grace. For I love you and long to give you My best. All I ask for this is a surrendered and willing channel for Me to live fully within.

Try Me in this and see My glory come forth in ways you have never known.

> *Flesh gives birth to flesh,*
> *but the Spirit gives birth to spirit.*
> *John 3:6*

MY PEOPLE ARE FREE

You are not a prisoner—do not act as if you still are.

Christ has set the captives free and you are free indeed. Do not let the devil deceive you into believing you are bound. I have given you the keys to be loosed from all your chains forged in this life.

Even in the times you appear imprisoned, I say "you are free." Like Paul and Silas, though in jail, their freedom was there all the time. And as soon as they acted on the grace apportioned them for that situation, down came the walls, and the enemy scattered. Are you any less than they as God's children?

I long to keep you free so you can take the keys of freedom to them that are still truly bound.

My people are free, they are joyful, able to enjoy life as I have created it to be lived. Walk in your freedom—stand tall.

If there's one thing I need for My flock, it is that they be free—free to love, serve, and obey. For it is in this freedom that I can know you and see you and you can experience My life for you.

It is for freedom that Christ has set us free.
Galatians 5:1

An Instrument of Power

I am strength in the midst of My people.

I will always show Myself mighty in a prayerful community of believers.

If only you knew the power of your intercession, how it destroys the powers of darkness, for this is My gift, Heaven sent, an instrument of power I have entrusted to each of you.

There is nothing I won't do when My people pray, for you join with the heavenly hosts in trampling the plans of hell.

My will has its way wherever it is exalted and presented amidst the earthly realms. Know there is nothing, absolutely nothing I won't do in the prayers of the faithful.

Let go in your trust of Me and let Me into that situation that calls for My power.

> *Where two or three come together in my name,*
> *there am I with them.*
> *Matthew 18:20*

I Am Your Source

Take your attention off the things of this world for they are passing away. I have eternal riches that far outweigh those earthly concerns you so often set your heart upon. I will give you what you need in your life on earth, but never let it substitute for what I want for you. Be careful, for the replacement of Me as your sole provider can be subtle. At any time you should be ready to let go of everything you have for My sake. If not, you are holding on too closely to the things of the world.

What is it you are clinging to at the moment? Is it worth more than our relationship? Can you believe Me that I can provide better each and every time you let go of something? I can do that 100 times, 1000 times, forever. Then why do you fear letting go of anything? I am your source.

I live for you and I desire to see My best for you. But let Me be the determinant of what that is. My gifts are based on My eternal love for you. I give them with your eternity in mind for as this world passes away, I long to draw you closer and closer to the day you will see Me face to face. Live today for that day and know it will surpass all that you have known.

Seek first his kingdom and his righteousness,
and all these things will be given to you as well.
Matthew 6:33

RIVER OF ABUNDANCE

There is nothing I wouldn't do for you when you come in the humility of love and service to My Kingdom. Too often you come asking amiss of My truest will for you.

Let My Spirit discern your motives and let your heart be purified. Then come and fulfill My Word, "ask and you shall receive." I long for My Word to come alive in the world for it has every power of Heaven behind it to reach its fulfillment in your life. Come, come and drink of the river of life. Its abundance awaits your every need.

The more you can let go of, the more I can provide. I can't fill clenched hands. Let go of that which you believe is so dear. I can replenish anything lost and make it better than it was before. I can, I will give you much more than your limited imagination allows or even seeks. You do not know My limits, for I have none.

Believe for Me to overflow you as you need and beyond. Why wouldn't I do this for those I call My own and love? Keep Me first in all things—your finances, your work, your family—everything and there is nothing I won't add to you.

I remind you to fan into flame the gift of God,
which is in you through the laying on of my hands.
II Timothy 1:6

My Promises

Your faith and trust in Me is a gift, one given to help you survive the times between My promises and their fulfillment in manifestation.

So often, you feel alone and ask "Where did you go, Lord? Where is that promise?"

I have not forgotten My promise to you even if you choose to shelve it for the mere fact that you are so troubled by standing and staying with it. The devil lives to steal promise. All perish without hope and promises of God give you that hope.

It is My grace that delivers the promise; it is My sovereign will that brings it to fruition. What, I ask, are you fearful of? My promises are meant to build your faith, not tear you down as you impatiently look for My hand of grace.

Your life is a promise—one that I knit together long before you had time to worry about it. You play a part in its coming to pass, but only to the extent that I allow it. So cherish the gift of faith I send you as we stand together in My covenant promises.

Your faith and belief will sustain you as you flow toward the promises I AM has set before you. There is only one direction for you and that is forward into the fulfillment of the fruit of My Spirit. Fear not—only believe.

Before My promise for you arrives, consider this: Are you willing to make the necessary changes to receive it? Do you have a grateful heart to which to welcome it? Are you willing to surrender your meager expectations for a Heaven-sent gift? Do you really desire this or are you too comfortable with not enough? Is your lack of patience a signal to Me that you'd rather settle for less now than wait for an awesome God?

> *You know with all your heart and soul*
> *that not one of all the good promises*
> *the Lord your God gave you has failed.*
> *Every promise has been fulfilled.*
> *Joshua 23:14*

GOD OF LIGHT AND DARK

Give 'til it hurts! Don't look for the light—be the light.

I am calling you out into My light, but first you must pass through what seems like utter darkness to get there. What you don't know won't hurt you; all you do need to know is Me. I am the God of the light and the dark.

Follow the darkness until you see My light, then you will know without doubt or reservation, it is I who calls you and is drawing you beyond the darkness into a marvelous light, the same light that drew wise men, that transfigured Moses, that calls down the centuries to all of My people.

"The night will shine like the day, for darkness is as light to You." (Psalm 139:12)

So often My requests of you come to you in the dark, seemingly without plan or reason. But each step of faith brightens the dimness. Do not be paralyzed by questioning or fearing what you don't see. For it is only the steps into the seeming abyss that cause My light to radiate.

Step forward into each new day, each day a new step bringing you closer to Me and further along in My call. "The steps of the righteous are ordered of God." You need only step them, for "I make straight the path."

This is not an easy command, but those who fail to heed it remain frozen in the space of indecision, unfruitfulness, no direction, and ultimately sorrow and anguish.

I call My people, all of them, daily, but they must come forth. I am ever there, but they must come forth. I am ever there, searching for they that come; and those I see, I promote.

You have few options in the Christian life: answer your call in Me or die on the vine. Is it worth the price, the pain, the momentary inconveniences? Settle for nothing less than My perfect calling. Your righteousness in Me will guide your steps, so stay close to Me always.

I am your God and I will *never* let you down.

> *If I say, "Surely the darkness will hide me*
> *and the light become night around me,"*
> *even the darkness will not be dark to you;*
> *the night will shine like the day,*
> *for darkness is as light to you.*
> *Psalm 139:11-12*

LIGHTING THE DARKEST HOUR

Yours is not a battle with your obstacles, but a challenge of your faith. You look to the obstacles and you doubt. Your fears overcome you, but it is really Me you question. You wonder, "Will the Lord really do this for Me? Can he do it? Does he have enough?" But why do you question Me when I don't yet have your full surrender? When will you be ready to lean your full weight upon Me?

Your powerlessness over your situation is a call to faith, a check of our relationship and how much you will trust Me in the darkest hour. You must put faith in something, be it Me or your fears. Even your fears are unknown, so why won't you turn to an awesome God who, you know, is fully capable and willing to serve your deepest, unknown needs?

Overcome yourself by surrendering in Me and I will not disappoint for I will light your way where you fear and bring you into an abundance as you have not seen. Trust Me.

"And I said to the man who stood at the gate of the year, 'Give Me a light that I may tread safely into the unknown.' And he replied, 'Go out into the darkness, and put your hand into the hand of God. That shall be to you better than light, and safer than the known way.'" (*The Gate of the Year*; Minnie Louise Haskins)

Then the Lord answered Job out of the storm...
Job 38:1

NEW LIGHT

Yes, together we shall bring forth Kingdom light and love. Let it shine! Let it reign!

Give yourself fully over to Me. Let your weakness become My strength. Surrender your helpless feelings and be confident that they are your hope to recognize your weakness and inability—and are actually the starting points for My grace. And be fruitful every day. Don't slip but once.

All I call My people to involves devotion and commitment, a true dying to self. Marriage, children, work—anything with worth involves work, but the payoff is substantial: a life that flows in the comfort and ease of knowing I'm with you in all things, that My will is being carried on through you and in you—just as I have purposed in since I created you.

Live for Me, day to day and know the "years teach much which the days never know." In spite of it all, press onward. Keep faithful to your calling and I will bring the Light.

> *Try Me in this and see if I will not throw open*
> *the floodgates of Heaven.*
> *Malachi 3:10*

BREAKTHROUGH

I am the God of the breakthrough. Of your breakthrough. Are you willing to bear with Me to see its fulfillment? For this could take most of a lifetime. Do you still want to bear with Me?

Is it the perceived breakthrough you seek or will you know when I get through to your situation? How often we seem to part ways when your expectations meet My intercession. Perhaps it was not what you expected. Then what does that say to you? "Where were you when I created the heavens and the earth?" Is My intervention, My way, in My time not enough for your situation of which I am fully and presently aware? One falters as a mortal when one questions where it is I am going.

That is why I have given a precious gift of faith. Faith reaches out to Me, beyond the circumstance of your days. You are all only the poorest of mortal beings when you bypass the avenue of faith and trust that leads back to My awesome presence, where all troubles and fears melt away.

I know it is hard and difficult for you to attempt to see who I really am and how I control this universe. But I have tried to assure you that you need not understand it, only believe in the fact that I control it in a loving realm. Therefore, I know what a breakthrough is and exactly when and where you need one.

Your Christian life is a breakthrough, a celebration, a victory, a light in the darkness, for in Me, your Savior, there is only rejoicing.

I am beyond it all and from where I see it, you could not be in a better place. And with faith and belief as your guide, you can join Me in this satisfying presence that knows only peace.

And, yes, you are free to come and escape to your peace.

He is not here—he has risen!
Luke 24:6

Thankful for My Bounty

A grateful heart is an open heart, fertile to receive more of My ever-flowing riches. Why count what you don't have when already you have so much? To be grateful for who I am for you pleases Me. It tells Me you are tuned in to the heart of God, recognizing My provision and encouraging you toward My future bounty.

For if you know what I have given you, where I have taken you from, and acknowledge My grace has taken you there, then it will lead you into a deeper faith that I am coming again like a river that never stops.

When you become faint of heart and are not thankful for My bountiful blessings each and every day you will begin to falter in your belief that I am a bountiful God who longs to shower My people with abundant riches.

And all I have for you is a gift freely given. Therefore, it is incumbent on you that you freely receive, for you cannot give thanks for that which you have not received.

A lack of gratitude will lead you down a path of self-entitlement, the thought that you are owed something from Me. Freely I give, for My supply is infinite.

And most important, I give you My love, the greatest gift I can give you, for it opens the door to you and I becoming one body, one Spirit.

None of My giving is earned—it comes from My essence in the day that I first formed you in perfect love, knowing I would never leave you abandoned or forsaken.

I love you and will always give you what I know you need in My wisdom, in My time, through you may never fully understand. Just believe in My love, freely receive it, and give thanks always for the endless flow of My grace for you.

> *Whatever you do, whether in word or deed,*
> *do it all in the name of the Lord Jesus,*
> *giving thanks to God the Father through him.*
> *Colossians 3:15-17*

A Relationship

I long to meet with you, to commune with My people.

It is more about our being one than it ever is about what you're doing for Me. Let that stem from our union, for nowhere else can you know the depth of My call on your life and where I want you than in the time we spend together.

Wasn't the cross about opening the way between us, so we could spend eternity together in the love of the Father, Son and Spirit?

All I do for you is My way of reaching out, drawing you in calling you My own. I will never bless where it is not My intent to bring us closer.

Within My blessings for you, please do not lose sight of Me. This life is about a relationship: yours and mine.

I long for all My people—the entire earth and everyone in it—to know Me, to know I love them passionately.

When our relationship is strong, it breeds a multiplicity of fruit: fellowship with your brothers and sisters; deeper joy; the ability to trust Me more; healing; a richness to all you do each day; a desire to serve; a hatred for sin; and peace knowing you are eternally loved.

Seek Me first in everything. See Me everywhere. I am with you always and My love never escapes you.

Come and partake of this banquet of grace I have for you right here, right now. I long for you. Hear My voice and answer My plea.

He is mine and I am his; he browses among the lilies
Song of Songs 2:16

I AM

My essence is in being, in I AM, not I DO. For you to be, involves the steady flow of My life in and through your very being. Is there anything you can do or enact that will ever shine brighter than who you already are in Me?

More of Me flows through surrendered vessels than you realize. My presence overwhelms—it is enough to create great changes in hearts and minds everywhere. It is My presence that drives those who turn away from Me to suffer needlessly, for they are turning into harm's way. Imagine he or she who flows into Me. Your thoughts, your words, your presence, and ultimately your actions are overshadowed by My Spirit in all you are. Why do you still strive for more of Me? You have Me, My children, for what father does not lend his all to his children?

Remember, less of you brings more of Me. Your "you," as My follower, is Me. It is Me in you. There is so much more I can and will do in you, when you strive less. I go to the depths of your being for you were created by Me for Me. I know who you are and why I created you. Rest in this truth and let your being fill up and overflow, for it is then that your doing will prosper and bring forth blessing and fruit.

God said to Moses, "I AM WHO I AM."
Exodus 3:14

BEYOND TRUSTWORTHY

I am Jehovah Jireh. I provide. Period.

You must learn to trust Me before you can actually trust Me to provide your every need.

I will teach you and show you the way, for it is in your relating to Me that the key to understanding what truth there is in trust. Trust involves thy very being. It is a bond, a covenant of truth, the essence of My very being.

Do not place your trust in Me as if you were trusting man, for I AM. You don't place trust in Me, for that involves too much of you. I am beyond trustworthy, for I am the Lord.

My words are beyond question. They need only to be taken and lived by those who truly know Me.

Remember My love for you transcends your understanding and it is the vehicle by which I make you like the Son.

Abraham called that place Jehovah-Jireh
(The Lord Will Provide)
To this day it is still said,
"On the mountain of the Lord provision will be made."
Genesis 22:14

Reliance on Me

Reliance means to "bind fast." It isn't faith until you rely on Me for everything.

Your tension and anxiety points to a lack of faith and trust in Me. Why else would you stress? I will show you the path.

Listen: no expectations should be Great Expectations.

I will put you in a position of complete reliance where I will take you through. There'll be no other way from now on.

Reliance on God is a great thing for it manifests Me in your life in magnificent ways. It is the route to My awesomeness in a victorious Christian life.

Stop settling for average. It doesn't cut it if you want to move onward in your journey. Dare to believe.

> *We know and rely on the love God has for us.*
> *I John 4:16*

TRUST ME

Anxieties, fears, trepidations, hesitations—often you let these define you.

You search for the familiar in the unfamiliar and you do not find peace. I have placed you where you will be fully reliant on Me to deliver to you My promises. I need only your trust that I am taking care of you.

Not only that, I am giving unto you to be a carrier of My grace to those around you. There is much to be added and much to be taken away. Your confidence in Me will grow with each time you release into Me.

Do not wallow in your search for the earthly comfortable, as it will only create further disdain. I am and always will be your source, your life, your purpose for being.

Begin anew looking to Me for your new life and see what wonders I will bestow. You need only trust Me.

*Trust in the Lord with all your heart
and lean not on your own understanding;
in all your ways acknowledge him,
and he will make your paths straight.
Proverbs 3:5-6*

I AM THERE WITH YOU

Submit to Me—release what you have and let Me in to commune with you. Let us be present to each other. In a spirit of submission, seek My wisdom and I will give you all you need to know for your situation. Then simply obey what I tell you to do based on My Spirit's direction.

You need only slow down long enough to receive from Me. Listen with your heart, clear your head, your mind of worldly clutter. Then simply let Me into your heart. There I will dwell and will work My ways through you. Submit. Seek wisdom. Obey.

I am there with you and will show you the way. How can I exist within you without bringing you truth and light? It is there for the asking. Seek it with all your heart for "the Lord is a rewarder of those who diligently seek him."

*When you seek me with all your heart
I will be found by you.
Jeremiah 29:13-14*

I Answer You

Listen to Me for I am speaking to My people always. I do not remain silent when you call, for I answer all My people.

Are you listening? Or is there something in the way? What is it you want to hear? Is not My truth enough for you?

It is contained in My Word. It comes in prayer, in the words of others who seek Godly counsel.

Like the wind, you know not the way My Word, My leading will come to you. Have you pre-conditioned how it will look? Be open to Me always, for it is an open heart that is able to hear and receive from Me. I will find you at your need and I will be your road, your light, your song in the night. As My love is revealed to you, so is My Word and My words. Do not hide from or shun what I say, for truth is evident to the Spirit-led one who listens to Me in the heart first.

I am your guiding light through this maze you know as your life. I do not expect you to go it alone which is why I am with you always. How could I not lead My people in the way they should go? Surrender your will as My Son, Jesus, did and believe Me to guide you into a far greater truth than you will ever know from your own actions.

Consider carefully how you listen.
Luke 8:18

Sweetness in Your Days

Do not look to the world for your validation, for your entire worth is found in your connection to Me.

Seek to praise and worship Me in all things; for it is in praise and worship that you will see beyond the temporal and peer into eternity where all earthly things fade away. The way to taste the sweetness of your days is to be heavenly-minded.

Seek My face now and in everything you are. For it is only through Me that anything will exude joy and light.

Grow beyond the shadows of the material things you hide behind and open up your heart to the Light of the World. I AM has come—He is here. Today. For you.

Take Me into your heart and praise Me 'til your joy begins to overflow, that others may know Me.

Joy can be yours everyday when you seek and discern My presence in all you do. Wipe free the tears for your savior has arisen today in your heart. Let it shine forth.

I have come that you may have life
and have it more abundantly.
John 10:10

JOY ETERNAL

Where is the joy in you that is so much a part of Me? As you fix your gaze on the earthly and temporal, you are bound to lose My joy.

There are enough desperate events in this life to keep you despondent throughout its duration. Where, then, is your hope and joy?

My joy is enduring and eternal. Where are you most focused? Check your relationship with Me: are you fully intent on our fellowship? Are you giving Me your time? Your mind and thoughts?

> *Restore to me the joy of your salvation.*
> *Psalm 51:12*

LOVE MY PEOPLE

Where is it you seek My goodness?

Do you see Me in the same places Christ sought his people? Amidst the lost, the broken, the downtrodden, the unrepentant, malicious, slanderers, those who have wronged you? Do you see Me also amidst your Christian brothers and sisters who you feel "don't get it"?

Do you see Me within yourself when you don't feel worthy or feel far from My plans for your life?

What do you expect Me to look like? And where do you expect Me to dwell?

For you who carry My Spirit, wherever you are, there I dwell. You always have enough of Me in you to make an immediate impact on your world.

Ask Me for the opportunity to move among the lost and the least. Do not do the choosing of who is worthy for I call all to My shadow of redemption.

Let others see My face through you.

For I still call others to you many times to open your eyes to My words. Do not be like Jonah and run from the "unworthy". Vengeance is mine alone in My time at My call.

But I do give you My mercy, My compassion, My vision—to receive and then to give. "Freely you have received, freely give." (Matthew 10:8)

I have called you to go out into all the world to every one. Remember, My will is for all to come to glory.

So you have My commission and My will to go with you. Now I need your heart, open and free, to love Me by loving My people.

But whoever has the world's goods and sees his brother in need,
and shuts up his heart from him
how does the love of God abide in him?
I John 3:17

The Higher Calling

You need to release that part, that thing you continue to cling to. It has no place in My Kingdom work. It only gives place to the work of the adversary. You must let it go and not dabble into anything which you may consider insignificant or OK, when, deep down, as you spend time in My presence, you know better.

"The devil seeks whom he may devour." And all of the Body is on his list. The devil is insidious—he will start small and take the ground inch by inch until he has you in a stronghold. Then you will be in bondage.

Do not stray from the way you know to be right—ever. Each day, each moment offers a choice—the way of good or the way of evil. And you have My light to guide you in everything. Consider your actions before you commit to them. Will your action exalt God? Or will you need to repent of it later?

Stand by your higher calling to the ways of Jesus Christ, for the standard of your Christian life has been set very high, yet not unattainable. Seek always the high road, though it may likely be the more difficult one. I need strong troops for the battles this life unfolds. Stay alert and do not let the slow moral decay of indifferent surrender take you down to the point where you cannot, or worse, will not, answer Me when I call you.

As you have therefore received Christ Jesus the Lord,
so walk in him
Colossians 2:6-7

BE FERTILE

Position yourself to receive the supernatural overflow of divine blessing.

Too often My people underestimate My ability and even more, My desire to bless My people.

Find yourself in the places where I have called you—in prayer, in praise, in worship, in obedience to My loving will for your life. And there you will see the blessings of My promise, covered in My never-ending agape love I have for each of you.

Be fertile ground for My gifts I'm longing to place in you.

Do not allow any earthly thing to stand in the way of us for nothing compares to the joy we have when we're connected in the freedom of a true love.

*Still other seed fell on good soil, where it produced a crop—
a hundred, sixty or thirty times what was sown.
Matthew 13:1-9*

THE HARVEST

You look for the harvest, but have you tended to your crops? Did you furrow the soil to create fertile ground, ready and open to be planted in? Did you pray for seed to plant? And, by the way, what about your neighbor's vineyard—is the soil of his/her soul any richer for what you've done for My Kingdom? What of the seeds of hope you planted? Do you trust that time will bring forth the fruit you and I so desire for your life?

Harvest never just happens—it is always happening.

Tending the soil, planting, watering, fertilizing: preparing and cleansing your heart, "Blessed are the pure in spirit for they shall see God"

Receive resources I send your way as seed, though they may look so small as a seed. Consider every Sequoia tree started as a seed.

Life comes by praising and worshiping Me for who I am; standing on My Word, the ultimate truth that brings living water; and standing and abiding in My presence, letting My love live and breathe in you and through you.

Your harvest is simply the by-product of a faithful and obedient Christian life. I have set it all before you today and everyday. Be faithful. Abide in Me.

Your harvest is a natural part of all Christian living and will come to bear on all the faithful who stand and persevere in the ways of My Word.

For it is the truth of life that transforms who you are and where you are going.

> *The seed on good soil stands for those*
> *with a noble and good heart,*
> *who hear the word, retain it, and by persevering*
> *produce a crop.*
> *Luke 8:15*

SOUL GRASP

Be watchful where you seek your security.

It is all too easy to seek the concrete elements of the world and build a shaky fortress. But it will not withstand the toughest challenges you face.

For a time, you will feel alive and strengthened by a stronghold of your own creation, but as you trust in that worldly element more and begin to lean on it with more of your reliance, you will begin to see how no man-made shield can truly protect you.

Begin to trust in Me more by letting go of each area you hide behind or cling on to. It is like the difference between grasping a piece of driftwood in high seas and being on board the largest sailing vessel.

As you let Me in and clear the path of earthly holds, I become ingrained into your way of being.

My power works eminently greater in every area where you previously relied on shallow, empty ways.

Your soul will grasp what your eyes can't see.

Everyone who hears these words of mine
and puts them into practice
is like a wise man who built his house on the rock.
Matthew 7:24

YOUR FORMER SELF

The challenging places I have called you where you are especially weak and challenged do not necessarily point to a greater sinfulness or personal inadequacy. Remember, it is I who called and lead you there to such a place where you see your limits and the weakness of your flesh. Here you are forced to rely on Me for your direction, your total reliance, not just your help.

I am with you to take control of your life as you willfully surrender more of yourself. It is here you must meet the cross and die to all traces of self if you are ever to bear fruit. I am the tree of life and it is from the tree the fruit is produced.

Thus, you must come to Me with nothing. Yet, if, at this point, you look at yourself and not to Me, you will see a helpless, needy mortal. It is at this seemingly meager point that the obstacles to a reliant life begin to peel away. Here, in contrast to your empty self, you will see more brightly your savior and hear more clearly My voice.

Know that it is My love that sustains you. Do not mourn the demise of your former self. Let loose the shackles that held you. Step over the walls that separated us. Come into My loving presence and be with Me. "He must increase, but I must decrease." (John 3:30)

Put on the new self
Ephesians 4:24

Resurrection Awaits

Empty yourself out, for I have come to fill your empty places. Gone are the old wineskins, and I have created a clear, new vessel where I can pour forth My anointing.

I have longed to place within you more of My Spirit, but together we have traveled down a seemingly long road of affliction, pain, remorse and struggle. At times you have asked, "where are you, Lord?" yet I have been with you guiding your steps through the maze of confusion and emptiness. I have done this to bring you to a place where less of you allows more of Me.

Remember, it is I who have come that you may have life more abundantly. This is My quest for you, not that you suffer and burn out on life, but that you and I bear up under the struggles and come forth proclaiming victory.

The way of the cross always leads you down a rocky path, but in the end, it will bring you to that place where you'll know it was Me, your Lord, that delivered you there.

Resurrection awaits—know that all your challenges and seeming defects are taking you to higher ground.

If we have been united with him like this in his death,
we will certainly also be united with him in his resurrection.
Romans 6:5

FREEDOM IN THE SPIRIT

You have a freedom in Me that you will know in no other way. "Whom the Son sets free is free indeed."

What is often defined as freedom is actually bondage to self. Wants, desires, and needs fulfillment do not necessarily define freedom.

You are free to the extent you choose to obey My will for your life. That is true freedom, unburdened by the limits of sheer human thought and cravings.

Each time you heed My call in your life, you grow closer to a more perfect life, one that greater reflects the image of My Son.

Ironically, this freedom has restraints—restraints on your flesh, your will, your plans, your presumptions of what your life "should" look like as you alone have perceived it.

Submission to Me is freedom and the more you let go of on this earth, the more freed up you will be to grow toward the Spirit.

*The Lord is the Spirit,
and where the Spirit of the Lord is, there is freedom.
II Corinthians 3:17-18*

All Things Are In Motion

Must you see everything to believe I'm doing a work in and around you? Is a tangible presence the only indication I'm working all things out for good? I have told you "I am with you always" and this encompasses every moment.

So much happens around you in nature that you don't notice, but see in the eventual passing of time: The grass grows and withers, waters evaporate, the sun sets. All things are in motion with Me.

I hear your prayers, I see your whole life, and My supreme knowledge works out all the details, including and especially the many you don't see or realize, much as in nature. Yet, you often "sense" nothing is happening. Do you really believe that?

Your lifetime in eternity terms is so short and I have much to accomplish within the time I have assigned you. Thus, no time is ever wasted. This is why I call you to a life of constant prayer, praise, and worship.

Each time you enter into My presence, I have something more to reveal to you, from the simplest "I love you" to profound directions for your life.

You'll always hear Me whenever you look for Me.

If you claim you're "not hearing"—how diligently are you seeking? I am at your every call, longing to impart My wisdom, joy, peace, hope, salvation—whatever you need, whenever you need it.

Come to the well of life and drink deeply.

*My Father is always at his work to this very day,
and I, too, am working.
John 5:17*

Heaven's Storehouse

I have a river of resources for all My people to draw from, an abundant flow of grace, so full of power, so rich and deep, a vast ocean of resources in every area for your life.

Call on My love and I will send you My Son to free you, heal you, and to bring joy and peace to the darkness of the world where you live now. Seek My healing—and I can stop disease, restore limbs, bring sight to the blind, raise the dead.

Seek My provision and I will bring a hundred circumstances into line in a matter of hours or minutes and take you to such abundant provision for exactly what you need, just when you need it.

When you seek My knowledge and wisdom, I can use you as a vessel to speak words of truth, to devise solutions to your problems, to set the captives free.

I have the storehouse pouring out and overflowing with Heaven's resources for the world's every need.

Don't ever think I Am is unable or unwilling. You are My vessels, My avenues of this storehouse to bring Heaven alive to this earth today. How "big" is your faith?

Come closer to Me and allow Me to work in you, for I am calling every day to manifest My presence.

Believe in the power of who I am and humble yourself to receive and let flow all I long to pour out in you and through you.

The Lord will open the heavens, the storehouse of his bounty.
Deuteronomy 28:12

Transformed in Me

I am ever transforming you from glory to glory as you yield your ways to My Word.

How easy it is to be conformed to the world around you despite the Spirit that resides within you. It would seem My light in you is enough to keep you on track, but we both know that is not always true.

Nevertheless, I am ever in you and with you.

Yet, your will plays a part in both the transforming and the conforming. Which will it be today?

The easy way of conforming lacks the challenge of turning away and freely taking the higher road of the leading of the Holy Spirit. Each surrender of your will to the leading of the enemy makes your next surrender that much easier and finding your way back to Me that much more difficult.

But I am here, always awaiting your turning back to Me. It is your choice.

I plead with you today—come, "be transformed by the renewing of your mind."

There is always a more excellent way through this life and it so often occurs in the seemingly simple daily choices.

Come, be transformed, lest you be conformed.

Do not lose sight of Me and begin to fall away with your poor, misguided choices.

Rely on Me and you know I will lead you by the hand to a way that will show you righteousness, joy, and peace as you shine forth My light.

Be transformed by the renewing of your mind.
Romans 12:2

TRUST IT ALL

Being in the right place for My timing is so often a key to the release of a breakthrough in your life. Daily, I call you—go here, do this, don't do that, walk this way—and every step is a piece of the plan I have for your life. How is it you can ever consider these "insignificant" when "the steps of the righteous are ordered of God"?

I know the end from the beginning. Carefully, I construct your life amidst sin, disobedience, demonic interference, free will—so many seeming hindrances in your eyes. To Me, they are all part of the plan and this is why I seek your obedience, submission, and humility.

You know not the next step, yet I know them all in My infinite, loving wisdom. Who are you to say to a given event, "Wonderful" or "Terrible" when your vision is so near-sighted? I am working in all your situations no matter how they appear and I work only for your good. Because I love you and you are mine.

Can you not trust that today's valley leads to tomorrow's peak? In spite of all My people have done throughout time, I still deliver them for My glory. Don't think it's about you for it is only in your surrendering to Me that you'll overcome your weakened state and see My strength come through.

Trust it all—"the big picture"—to Me; for you'll never know today what glory I bring to your life in the seeming insurmountable circumstances you face.

Let your trust in Me be your guide, your source of comfort, your hope, for "weeping may endure for a night, but joy comes in the morning." (Psalm 30:5)

He makes me lie down in green pastures.
Psalm 23:2-3

Relinquish Control

Self-preservation is neither an aim nor an end. Its leading causes great consternation to the soul; its fruits are worry, fear, anxiety, selfishness.

When you feel the yearning deep inside upon facing a difficult situation, begin to seek the Spirit as to what is going on within you.

Man naturally seeks to protect the flesh, a mere image, so often just a pretense. And for what? And why? If you were to trust in My continuous, unending, diligent love for you, you would know I am there in the midst of it all.

I ask you to die to self not to be anxious in relinquishing your supposed control, but to clear the way for My Spirit to have dominion in you, producing peace, joy, and hope, wherever this life finds you.

Your control is a fantasy, an insidious tool of the enemy to keep you out of union with Me. Though temporary circumstances will imitate what you deem "being peaceful", it is only in your heartfelt surrender, your relinquishing of cares and concerns that you will know the one true source of light—Jesus Christ, your savior, your Lord, your brother, your beginning, your end, your all in all.

In his heart a man plans his course,
but the Lord determines his steps.
Proverbs 16:9

A Contagious Instrument

Be encouraged to be bold when you speak, for My Spirit resides within you. As you surrender your life and your days to My will, know that I will work My truth in and around you to touch others in ways you could not know.

My presence in you is the beginning of a proclamation of who I am to those who seek Me at all levels of need, directly and indirectly.

Your words are only a part of the truth of who I am—but it is your Spirit-filled being that shines My light.

Let your whole being embrace the truths of My Word—your words, your actions, your intercessions.

Speak the truth in love, be it comfort, correction, encouragement, joy, hope. Assume your surrendered vessel will be a contagious instrument to speak wisdom and truth. Therefore, speak forth the life within, no matter how small you may deem that to be.

With "I in you and you in Me" you are able to speak and act in My name.

Seek the Spirit and let your words and actions be heard, as you are lead.

> *May they be brought to complete unity*
> *to let the world know that you sent me*
> *and have loved them even as you have loved me.*
> *John 17:22-23*

THE WAY OF GOD

You always think "things could be better", but have you consulted with your Father, the one who discerns all things for you? You might think you have an idea, but, really, you are clueless.

I have come to show you truth and make you great in My sight. My greatness for you looks very much like nothing in your sight. Can you live with that? "The first shall be last." "He who humbles himself for My sake will be made great." When your life looks like nothing, it is then I am working most, to clear your vision to Me, lest you get caught up in your "successes" and how you did a wonderful thing. No, it is only I who does great and wonderful things in your Christian life.

Do you not know by now just how different My life for you is than the world's version? Very different.

Beware, if your life begins to look too much like the world's, for then, it is likely you have begun to shut Me out and do things on your own strength, seeking a more acceptable personal image in your sight. Care only for the things of My light. The rest are on shaky ground. What appears most solid in this world is the least of anything I would want you to entrust your life to.

And then there's the way of My God—it is a life most unacceptable to the masses. Who wants to die? Who wants or seeks to be the least? What grandeur is there in a cross?

Trusting in Me will bring you a way of life that all long for, yet wastefully seek in an ephemeral existence.

I alone can know for you peace and satisfaction within, that will have you to shine above the rest, for they will say, "What manner of man is he who takes counsel not among his peers, but knows and speaks of truth that few others dare speak?" Live for Me, love in Me, and you will know life, true life.

> *For whoever exalts himself will be humbled,*
> *and whoever humbles himself will be exalted.*
> *Matthew 23:12*

A New Sense of Delight

You run from the cross because you see it as hurt, pain, vulnerability. Have you ever thought of Me inside of that?

It is in your weakness, your dependence upon Me that you become effective—strong with calm and without pride; gentle, not defensive; vulnerable, softened to be shaped; weak, that you know clearly your many limitations. Yet you look at the limitations and feel weak.

Don't you know I come in when you and your petty show of "strength" are set aside? Your fortress that protects a you of your own creation, one that needs demolishing, not protection. I am your protection in the things that matter. Lay aside your fear, your apprehension.

Come to Me weak and on your knees with a new sense of delight that I am in you and that your sense of weakness is a reminder of whose you are. When the devil comes in at this time, you have My Word and My anointing. Hear Me alone. You're more afraid of the surrender of control than anything else.

> *This is a faithful saying:*
> *"For if we die with him, we shall also live with him.*
> *If we endure, we shall also reign with him.*
> *If we deny him, he will also deny us.*
> *If we are faithless, he remains faithful; he cannot deny himself."*
> *II Timothy 2:11-13*

THE LORD IS YOUR PORTION

You create your own void trying to fill the space of your life with something not of Me. Why? Put no vain idols before you—jobs, relationships, finances. Focus on My love. I am Jehovah Jireh, your Provider.

Look to Me anew each day for I have gifts that you see and many you do not see. This is My grace happening.

Walk by faith, not by sight. Leave your old way of thinking.

Come to a new place in Me, one that revives, that makes whatever you do have meaning because of Me.

His mercies are new every morning;
great is Thy faithfulness
'The Lord is my portion' says my soul,
therefore I hope in him!
The Lord is good to those who wait for him,
to those who seek him.
It is good that one should hope and wait quietly
Lamentations 3:23-26

A Shift in Life

Spend time with Me. Walk along side Me again, My friend.

Don't let the fears of your present circumstances cloud our connection. Your focus is off when you allow it in.

The most important thing is our time together. Here I speak unhindered by your "stuff", clear of your preconceived ideas and perceptions of life.

Letting Christ in is a radical step, so different from the life you've known. You should expect nothing less when I come in. How could My entry ever be anything you might conceive? How could it?

I am a radical transformer—I have come to make things new which means an end to the old, and a bold new way, a shift in life as you know it. Do not resist this, but trust it and give in to My ways.

It is clearly—from My view—a better life for you. Will you believe Me in this?

> *I run in the path of your commands,*
> *for you have set my heart free.*
> *Psalm 119:32*

WAIT FOR ME

I must manifest things in your life lest I am less real to you.

"I would have lost heart unless I believed I would see the goodness of the Lord in the land of the living." (Psalm 27:13)

Wait in faith on the Lord.

> *Be of good courage, and he shall strengthen your heart.*
> *Wait I say, on the Lord.*
> *Psalm 27:13*

GODLY PATIENCE

Is patience doing a perfect work in you? (James 1:4) The fruit of Godly patience allows you to stand in the days of trials and still rejoice in who I am, not wavering with fears, doubt, or dissatisfaction. You are My creation and I have styled you to be a beacon of light, joy, and hope, a reflection of the Savior.

Are there places in your walk that are lacking for want of the next desired goal? My perfect timing is what makes goals into blessings. And the time in between all of it coming to pass requires patience, steadfastness, and a perseverance to know Me more deeply.

When your yearning brings you pain and despair, consider you may have lost the sound of My voice drawing and encouraging you and instead, have begun feeding on the thoughts of the enemy who seeks your downfall. My Word tells you there is a season and a time for every purpose. (Ecclesiastes 3:1) How long will you bear up under your circumstances? As long as you walk by sight and not in faith, you are likely to know despair.

Ask yourself why is it you can't be patient with Me. Have you a better plan that more readily meets your desire? Beware the leanness of soul that awaits those who seek quail in the desert. (Numbers 11) Impatience only leads to murmuring and complaining—ultimately, dissatisfaction and doubt toward your Lord.

Abide in the vine and let Me take up your yoke. Know that I will find a way for you, a way you would never know outside of your surrendering to Me. Do not weary yourself in self-controlled endeavors that are not of Me.

Seek My face and I will lead you. And if you must wait awhile, stand strong and "lean not on your own understanding" (Proverbs 3:5)

Let Godly patience be the measuring stick of your trust in Me, the one who delivers you and lifts you up.

Love is patient.
I Corinthians 13:4

BE STILL

Be more caught up in Me than in your works for Me. Your actions will flow to the degree My presence is found within. Do not look for the work to do nor look for the task of service. Start with seeking My face, My heart.

I long to be "Christ in you", but it is a challenge when you're too busy to commune with Me and in Me. I can maximize your ministry to the extent that you take the time to hear Me and know just what to do as I have ordained it. When you are present with Me, you will know and sense the confidence that comes from being truly and deeply loved.

Consider how often you fail to act out of fear, timidity, self-consciousness, self-righteousness, imitating others, following the crowd, laziness, or just no zeal to minister. What if you were so close to Me, so ingrained, so much enjoined and enmeshed with My Spirit, that anything of this world did not distract you? What would you be capable of at this point?

The interaction between the Father and the Son, that oneness—that's what I desire for us.

A submitted self is what I can work in and through: your receiving, My infilling and overflowing. This is how I touch the world—My love in you lighting the way with the passionate driven love of the Savior.

> *The Lord will fight for you; you need only to be still.*
> *Exodus 14:14*

Draw Near to Me

In your times of utter helplessness where you see no light amidst the darkness all around you—what do you do? Where will you go? The darkness has a way of becoming all-consuming. Is your situation beyond what you could ever imagine it to be like differently? I am a powerful, almighty God and I equip My people for freedom to love and to be loved. My plan never involves your oppression. I tell you to press in and draw near to Me.

Come, praise Me. At times, enact warfare prayer against the forces of the enemy that hold you and this world down. Prayer and fasting will put your focus back upon Me.

At times of duress, it is so human to seek one's own needs and to try to meet them in so many ways that never fulfill: avoidance, escape, worry, controlling, complaining, blaming. These are beyond you for it is not about you.

You are My vessels created by Me for honor and to share My glory. Amidst sorrow, in Me you'll find joy; in fear, I am your protection; in loneliness, I am your ever-loving companion and friend; in pain, your healing balm who comforts; in confusion, I am your wisdom. Consecrate yourselves toward Me in the most difficult times.

Draw near to God and he will draw near to you.
James 4:8

THE PRESENCE

Come and join in the presence of the throne of the Lamb of God with all his angels—rejoice, let go of all your temporal troubles for "in My presence is fullness of joy." (Psalm 16:11)

Let go all self-concern and consciousness of how you look or how others may see you. You are called first and foremost to holiness and to find your source of strength, peace, hope, and love in Jehovah God.

I am your all in all, more awesome than the most wonderful, awe-inspiring aspects of My creation. I love for you to enter into My presence in praise and thanksgiving. It is here you begin to see Me more for who I am, to glimpse the heavenly eternal, a joyful place so far removed from the suffering and evil in the world today.

I need for the body to catch sight, to taste the greatness that is yours in Christ Jesus your savior and lover and protector of your soul. When you sense where you stand in My eyes, you will know you are loved to the core of your being.

I am so much a part of you: your next breath, your next step, inhabiting your thoughts, reaching to the essence of who you really are. For I created you to be loved by Me in a way you couldn't possibly know in earthly measures. Once you have tasted the love I have for you, you will always yearn for more of Me. And I will keep filling you until the day I call you home.

Until then, I am with you always, loving you and longing for you to come and be filled with more of My Spirit here and now, so much so that you will be no stranger to Heaven when you arrive.

> *You have made known to me the path of life;*
> *you will fill me with joy in your presence,*
> *with eternal pleasures at your right hand.*
> *Psalm 16:11*

AMAZING FAVOR

Ask for it all. When you do, prepare your heart to receive. Do not hold back anything from Me—your praise, your asking, your confession, your love. I have overwhelming grace and provision for your every touch with Me. Give Me your all, not a tired glance.

Expect so much more from Me. Who are you to think that with any encounter with Me that this time will not be one of amazing favor? Amidst your asking, your seeking, you may already be deeply within My greatest abundance and loving will for your situation.

Judge not what your life should look like as you seek Me with a pure and earnest heart. Did I not spend many years shaping, molding, and preparing Moses, Daniel, Joseph, Peter, Paul? Was it more important how they turned out or how they grew in their struggles? And did you not see something in their story that built you up?

As I answer your call, I answer only with My best for you, My perfect will comes forth into your plea. I am consumed in your calling for Me. I assure you all of Me always. I am working a far greater thing in your life over time than any present moment may reveal. Just know I AM is there.

This is the confidence we have in approaching God:
that if we ask anything according to his will, he hears us.
I John 5:14-15

My Vision Within

Let no word come to your ear, no sight to your vision, nor let any thought enter your mind that would cause you hindrance to My vision of faith for you.

Sights and sounds cause reactions that can set you on a worldly course void of My direction. Maintain in My presence and hear My voice deep within.

"For those who live according to the flesh set their minds on the things of the flesh, but those who live according to the Spirit, the things of the Spirit." (Romans 8:5.)

You do not have to surrender to every wayward thought that comes your way each day. The devil knows your mind is a battleground to plant lies, doubts, deceptions, fear, hatred. Day by day, he attacks and takes every inch of ground you surrender by giving in and not standing on My truth, supernatural truth that brings life and light to your path.

"In Me you live and move and have your being." Live this truth. Stand on My words until you hear otherwise, but you'll never hear otherwise because My truth is eternally lasting and victorious.

For who among men knows the thoughts of a man
except the man's spirit within him?
In the same way no one knows the thoughts of God
except the Spirit of God.
I Corinthians 2:11

THIS SIDE OF ETERNITY

I seek your intentionality in all Godly pursuits. Standing in faith is not a passive activity, it is a daily, often hourly, abiding, standing, and believing for My continuous intervention.

So often when I act in the natural, it is the culmination of a diligent seeking, an intercession, a proclaiming of My Word into the seeming abyss of what appears to you a hopeless place.

I am ever working in your behalf as you present yourself to Me and seek Me throughout the time of your earthly life and the various trials it bears. As I've told you, I am with you always.

Come, now, today be with Me. Your circumstances are not the call to Me, but I desire you at all times. I will always fill you with more grace, blessings, joy, and anointing to bring deeper fulfillment in every area you encounter.

Come to Me fully expecting Heaven's outpouring, the fullness of Me, My promises. Expect no less—ever.

I have covenanted with My people to carry out great, awesome, wonderful things, both on this side of eternity and in the next. Bear with Me always and do not allow yourself to become a victim of your circumstances.

Know I am doing a mighty work and I never do one thing. My end results for your desires involve far more than what appears.

I am drawing you, deeply, into relationship, where My love will change you first. Realize this as you are tempted to murmur for what you deem lack of results. It is so much more.

As you seek My face, I will provide what I know you need as I have designed it in My loving plan for your life.

> *He has also set eternity in the hearts of men;*
> *yet they cannot fathom what God has done*
> *from beginning to end.*
> *Ecclesiastes 3:11*

I Will Never Let You Go

Have you ever considered how much of this life is about our relationship? The trials, the tests, the struggles, the learning through it all, the dying of the flesh: it all comes back to Me.

You see your struggles first, so often before you cut through them and see Me standing with you. I so long to be Lord of all, your everything, your passion.

If only you could love Me within a small fraction of how I love you, you would know true joy and peace in Kingdom living. You will know this more fully when we commune eternally in Heaven, so overwhelmed by My love it will overshadow every other thing as there will be nothing else. You will be caught up in the truest love of the Trinity.

But I tell you today you can taste of this love. I passionately desire to embrace you in the depths of your soul.

This is not earthly love as you may (or may not) know it. Earthly love starts at the mind level and tries to work its way inward. My love resonates from within at your human core and shines outward. Praise and worship bring it to light.

I want you so desperately and long to embrace you forever. Everything else is passing away, but our relationship is eternal. All you endure in this life is ultimately working together for your good (Romans 8:28) as you let it draw you closer to Me. Your will is the door to our intimate relationship.

Trust Me more deeply. For I have healing to restore you, forgiveness to redeem you, joy to uplift you, and the peace of Christ to give you hope. You are mine—always. Nothing will ever come between My love for you for it is never earned.

Let Me love you. Open your heart. Believe Me when I tell you this, nothing could be more true: I long for you, I love you, and I will never, never let you go.

His left arm is under my head,
and his right arm embraces me.
Song of Songs 2:6

Eternal Strength

Your human state is one of continual weakness. Your strength comes only from Me—why delude yourself into believing you can go it alone and "be strong"?

What you often deem strength is nothing less than standing on foundations of sand: temporary holds on this passing world, extant in your own mind and as fleeting as the thoughts that come and go.

My strength is eternal.

It brings peace, humility, and a deeper understanding that you are mine and I am yours. The devil will present to you "riches" of his inheritance that ultimately lead to destruction. ("Unless the Lord builds the house, its builders labor in vain." Psalm 127:1)

Do not accept a weak earthly substitute for My grace. Over-reliance on worldly comforts will only lead you to patterns of sin and deadly addictions. My comfort so often comes from the fleshly discomfort of the cross. If it is your flesh that seeks comfort, you must come unto Me and "be crucified with Christ". (Galatians 2:20)

Once you let go of what it is that drives you down the wrong path, you will see Me right before you, closer than you could have imagined in your most dour, dark moment.

I am never far away, though at times, you may think Me distant.

It is the distractions of the finite mind that hide Me.

Surrender to the truth of My omniscient, all-present being and see the face of the Father who longs to love you and comfort you. Let "the joy of the Lord be your strength." (Nehemiah 8:10)

> *The weakness of God is stronger than man's strength.*
> *I Corinthians 1:25*

THE GIFT OF GLORY

You wonder, "When will I see glory in this sinful body?" The habitual sins, the unholy attitudes, the thoughtless actions, the venomous words, the sporadic prayer times—how, you ask, can these still be so much a part of me when the Spirit of God dwells within?

Are you looking for proof of your righteousness? Maybe you don't feel redeemed. Despite your renewed spirit, you find yourself feeling almost "trapped" in your sinful flesh. How much personal growth must your see before you'll truly believe you are worthy?

Remember, it is in your weakness that My strength is made perfect. (II Corinthians 12:9) I will love you regardless of what you do for I love you for who you are and I love you exactly as I made you. You are lacking nothing in Me. I have given you My gift of unending forgiveness from the cross of Jesus. His blood covers all your sins—past, present, future. No sin is too great for the blood of the Savior.

Run to Me in your weaknesses and failings—let Me be your strength. You are broken and wounded in your flesh, a product of imperfect attempts at human, temporal, and conditional love.

I know this about you and have seen your life unfold in all its brokenness. My mercy is here for you.

You need never work up to a personal sense of goodness or feelings of being righteous. Come before Me today, just as you are. It is I who will work in you an "eternal weight of glory." Even your best works are passing away.

Refuse to live in the realm of condemnation where the devil yearns to take the world, especially believers in My name. You are redeemed, set free, My beloved.

Receive this truth and believe Me when I tell you how much I love you. "For we also are weak in him, but we shall live with him by the power of God toward you." (II Corinthians 13:4)

> *For our light affliction, which is but for a moment,*
> *is working for us a far more exceeding*
> *and eternal weight of glory.*
> *II Corinthians 4:16-17*

THE ONE WHO SEES ALL

I know the end from the beginning. I see everything that happens as a part of a complete whole. You do not possess this gift, but you possess the one who does.

Trust Me through it all, especially when you feel things "don't make sense". Within a limited viewpoint, when you can't see how the present ties into lifetime and eternal purposes and designs, it is easy to despair. I have planned this vast universe down to the smallest detail.

I am a God of details and I am intricately and lovingly putting together your life as you submit it to Me. And even when you don't, I will guide you toward My perfect will. I am ever interceding for you. It is pure joy to Me when My children prosper.

So often, the path to Godly prosperity is strewn with battles, trials, setbacks, failures. Remember, I told you that "in this world you will have tribulation." Didn't I also say, "Be of good cheer, for I have overcome the world"? (John 16:33)

No matter how much you believe you have "messed up" or missed it, I am greater than that belief, for I am your redeemer and can make any situation alive with My presence. And when some things happen even as you're "doing everything right"; still, rejoice, and know that I am God, a God of victory.

My truths are eternal and every day they bear upon your life through the dominion of the loving promises I have created for My family.

Trust the one who sees all and who loves deeply.

*In this world you will have tribulation,
but be of good cheer,
for I have overcome the world.
John 16:33*

A Heart of Flesh

What is it that has hardened your heart toward Me? Have you drifted down your own path of troubles, leaving Me in your wake? Keep a soft and tender heart towards Me always, for it is this place of connection with Me where you'll readily find Me when you seek Me.

Often, My "distance" from you has more to do with the hardened areas of your heart that will not be penetrated with My healing, joyous Spirit. You must enter into My presence to break the stoned out areas.

In what ways have I become secondary in your life? Where do I fall in your level of priorities? Are you passionately loving Me in your thoughts, prayers, and actions toward others? Your prayer times? Or, are you just "liking" Me as a casual acquaintance that you take for granted? How will I know you love Me? Do not take My love for granted for it is too precious, too powerful for your every need to make it merely lukewarm.

My love is a consuming fire that swallows you up and takes you to the heavenlies to share together with Me.

Love finds its fulfillment when it is shared in equal fervor. It can never truly be a one-way message.

Though I am always loving you and have always loved you, even when you did not know Me, I long for the fulfillment of our love when you come to Me as you are and love Me for who I am.

I have called you for a higher calling, one that is honorable and worthy of My name. Mediocrity and half-heartedness won't do for I reward those who "diligently seek" Me. (Hebrews 11:6)

You will eventually reap what you sow: weak prayer times, numerous small choices of your own will, un-confessed sin, demonic interference left unchallenged. Your inactivity and indifference in any of these areas will only feed your natural inclinations toward worldliness. Is this the life I have called My sons and daughters to? Not in the least.

I am serious about your call, your commission to do Godly endeavors. Is your vessel prepared at any given moment to answer My higher calling?

*I will give you a new heart
and put a new spirit within you.
Ezekiel 36:26*

MISSION OF AN ADULT

I am calling you to a maturity in your Christian life necessary to fulfill the wonderful plans I have set for you. "When you were a child, you talked, thought, and reasoned like a child. When you became a man, you put childish ways behind you". (I Corinthians 13:11)

Have you put your childish ways behind you yet? How often do you still seek your own way, not mine? To whom does vengeance belong? (Romans 12:19) Do "the lust of the flesh, lust of the eyes, and the pride of life" still dominate much of your world? (1 John 2:16) Do you freely and immediately forgive others as I have forgiven you? (Luke 6:37) Is My Word alive in your heart enough to truly be "a lamp unto your feet"? (Psalm 119:105)

You would not send a child out to do the mission of an adult. Nor will I. I give you the tools of perfecting your way—My Spirit, My Word, My spiritual gifts covered in My love and grace. They are yours for the asking with the submission of your heart to My will.

Do you not realize, your life is passing away as it is but "a breeze that does not return"? (Psalm 78:39) Spend it wisely. See and live what I have for you. Drink it in. All of it.

I never hold back toward My people whom I love. Do not hold back either. Open your heart to receive what I have for you.

Let My plan unfold graciously in your life. Take it in and pour it out to everyone whether they "deserve" it or not. Be Christ to one another. Become the Father to those in need. Let My Holy Spirit live in you today.

*But solid food is for the mature,
who by constant use have trained themselves
to distinguish good from evil.
Hebrews 5:14*

FREE OF STRIVING

At what point will your constant striving bring you the peace your heart desires? Letting go is always the first and wisest decision.

Not having peace is not an option for Kingdom living nor is it ever an end. Lack of peace is merely a signpost to point you toward My call for your life. I will lead you to a place of peace, hope, joy, but I will need your true surrender.

Do you feel as if you are striving in prayer? Have you come first to Me with open hands and a clear heart? Do you see Me for who I am, what I have given you, My all-knowing, all-loving, all-powerful being and My intimate connection to you? Or do circumstances and thoughts of past pain and projected, continued unrest dominate you?

Trust My timing, receive My promises, stay focused on the Heavenly vision. Call on Me at all times and I am with you. Keep surrendering, keep letting go.

Seek the cross and let your earthly desires for comfort, pride, control, revenge, indifference be laid before the cross. You are more free each time you give in to My ways, though your flesh will struggle against it.

The more you surrender each time, the more fruit will yield. Let this become a way of life, a new habit. As you feed your earthly desires less, though they may initially hunger for more, eventually, they will starve and you will see and know My peace, free of striving.

My Word says, "seek and you will find." Striving is a fruitless human endeavor that keeps man in control and it only begets greater striving. Let go of those areas that are weighing you down. Ingrain this practice into your soul. And see the fruit of the Spirit fill your life.

*I will cast my burden on the Lord
and he shall sustain me.
Psalm 55:22*

LET GO OF CONTROL

When I seek your full submission, your total surrender, I am looking for you to get out of the way for My abundant grace to follow. I need your fully letting go that clearly shows your willful intention is for Me to act.

So many times, your desire is for control, be it subtle or direct. This act of your will is subversive to My Kingdom flow. Great is the glory to Heaven when you allow awesome manifestations to infill your life. And mighty is the result of the fruit in your life.

You will see the power of Christ alive as you let Me operate freely. One of Satan's easiest, but most powerful tools, is to get you to feed into the lie that you must seize control and begin to take action on your own. Fear will instigate this as will pride, self-sufficiency, lack of faith in who I am.

I am Jehovah God, your infinite and loving provider, able to meet your needs in exceeding abundant measure (Ephesians 3:20)—if you allow Me to enter in. Don't be caught in Satan's trap.

So many of My people are desolate as they cling to their old selves, wondering, "When, Lord, will you answer me?" You hold the keys to so much of My outpouring when you trust Me. Have I not shown Myself trustworthy to tend to your every need?

I am the Christ who entered your world to be with you and My Spirit dwells within you. Trust Me. Let go. I'm here to catch you as you fall into My loving arms. Live in the freedom of depending solely on Me.

My grace is sufficient for you.
II Corinthians 12:9

Taste the Divine

What statement is your life making with regard to your relationship with Me? Is it an intentional act of moving ever closer to Me? Are you free? Free to love Me? Is the Christ in you evident to others? This life is about being in Me and with Me at all times. "In My presence is fullness of joy". (Psalm 16:11)

Are you spending enough time communing with Me—just you and I? I long to be with you. I want us to spend time together where you're not petitioning or seeking some earthly gain that you see as paramount. Too often those petitions overshadow Me.

You know I am the God who can make things new. But what I want is you. All of you. Can you still rest in Me when all about you appears in turmoil? Why does My Word speak of peace amidst tribulation? Were it not possible, it would not be there.

Spend some time with Me where you are alone with Me, just seeking My heart, resting in Me, letting go. I can refresh and bring light to your world just being with Me. Come in praise and worship. Fix your heart, soul, and mind on all things Godly. Pray for My heart and mind. I will be with you and I will speak to your heart. You will taste of My peace.

Give us some time—don't rush through our time as you might any other event in your day. Our time together is too important. Come, My child, and be present with Me. Taste the divine.

Let Me flow in you, over you, through you. Once you know this, you will begin to long for more.

And I will meet you each time. Trust Me. I will be there. I am there. My love is all-consuming. Let it consume you today.

Taste and see that the Lord is good;
blessed is the man who takes refuge in him.
Psalm 34:8

THERE IS NOTHING WE CAN'T ENDURE TOGETHER

Is the faith you have in Me just blind belief or is there more to it? What keeps your trust in Me thriving? Do you look for buds on the vine to energize you? And if you don't see them—then what? What is your faith in? Rather, who is it in?

True faith is designed to be in a person, the person of Jesus Christ. Anything less will be a product of you and woefully inadequate for where I've called you to go.

Like Peter, an incomplete focus on Me will cause you, too, to begin sinking, further debilitating your confidence. Though you may begin sinking, even then—especially then—reach out for Me and I will rescue you.

I am more honored by your willingness to step out of the boat where sinking seems a real possibility. But once out, you must not go back. Peter never looked to the boat for his refuge—he looked to his Savior.

I stilled the storm with a whisper. (Luke 8)

Is your mind and spirit so chaotic with the furious sounds of your difficulties that you fail to hear Me whispering peace to your storm? When will you trust Me? The alternatives are few. In fact, no human ones exist. Fear, frustration, endless pining, inner consternation—all reveal your heart. Can you see it? It's your chance to see what I see in challenging times. Run to Me for your refuge and I will heal you.

The real issue isn't your problem: You need Me more. Problems begin to fade when brought into My light.

I have internal answers (for your heart) as well as external resolution (for your situation) which you could never imagine in a lifetime of worry.

Let the truth of My Spirit set you free.

There is nothing you face too big for Me, nothing we can't endure together.

Keep your heart focused on Me for I will always lead you "through the valley of the shadow of death" to a joyful, hope-filled resurrection.

*In fear and amazement they asked one another,
"Who is this? He commands even the winds and the water,
and they obey him."
Luke 8:25*

BE READY

How long will you bide your time with Me? Don't you know I desire to bring My promises to you more than you're ready to receive them? Standing on My Word is not an easy thing to your flesh. In between the promise and its fulfillment, I am working much in you that is actually part of the promise.

How do you typically receive from Me? What do you expect? It seems My people often make in an issue of timing that challenges most their belief in My fulfillment of My Word.

Do you know this promise to you is for an appointed time? Have you prayed for it? Do you have a witness to My Word for you? Do you know deep in your heart that I have spoken, where it does not waver or go away and you know this is not something you came up with, but was planted by the Holy Spirit? If you know this, when you know this, as you know it is I, the Lord, who have spoken to you—then stand together with Me for the manifestation of My promise.

I have promises, plans for all My people. Do not waver from what you know is Me. Be prepared for the season of arrival. Be prepared for when My plans begin to unfold; you do not want to see them unfold while you're not ready because you doubted or did not take My call seriously.

I am the God of Heaven and earth who can make anything I choose unfold in your life. And it will all occur for your good. (Romans 8:28)

Do not fear what you are standing on is folly, for I will tell you and show you what is of Me and what is not. The strongest will can be enlightened by the grace I give.

My love for you is the driving force I use to open you up to receive good and wonderful gifts.

These promises ultimately have more to do with Me and My greater plan for the body of Christ, of which you are a vital part. Stand with Me and let Me be glorified in what I'm doing for you, in you, and through you.

> *Be ready, because the Son of Man will come*
> *at an hour when you do not expect him.*
> *Luke 12:40*

Look to Me in Awe

The vision of the Living God far surpasses what this earth can offer or provide for you to fully grasp.

Think big, truly beyond what you can even know.

The greatest things in nature—oceans, mountains, galaxies—only approach the awe-inspiring aspect of your God's nature.

I am beyond words and the wildest imagination. Do not let Me be imprisoned by your average thoughts. I am God, the most amazing being in existence.

Approach Me in praise to enter into My sanctuary. Here you will begin to sense who I am and how everything I do is awesome and mighty, from My love to My miracle-working intervention.

Absolutely nothing is beyond Me. Pray expectantly to Me for anything. Let Me be God, awesome in love and service and provision.

I am your all, your everything. Look to Me in awe and know that I am more than anything you'll ever see in this lifetime.

I long to unleash the power of Heaven in your life.

This is the God you should consider when you pray and praise. The one who is eternal and true. No problem you have is even close to a problem for Me. I am your answer.

Therefore, it is only your faith, your belief in My saying I am who I am that will enable you to come to Me as more than the God of your mind and experience. Always know that I am much more. Come to Me in full abandonment and you will see Me through the eyes of your heart.

Who is like you—
majestic in holiness, awesome in glory, working wonders?
Exodus 15:11

BEYOND YOURSELF

Remove the focus from self. Why be so consumed with the image you portray when the Lord looks to the heart? One of the biggest distractions you have to Me is the focus you keep on yourself.

I have so much in the supernatural that awaits your call, but what hinders it? Comfort zones, not being noticed, half-hearted commitment, lack of diligence—what is it for you that holds on to that sense of self you find so necessary to preserve?

Remember: your life is not your own. This means I seek abandonment in exchange for abundance. Never get too comfortable with who you think you are for at any given time, that is only a passing image.

You should be focused forward and on your way to ever greater Kingdom living. I have new revelation for you daily. Take in whatever you can to get closer to Me and receive the gifts that build the body of Christ.

Die to yourself daily, take up your cross—then you are ready to follow Me. (Mark 8:34-35) Don't miss Me. Get beyond yourself and you will be free to see Me and to see yourself in light of Me. The days are short and your eternity awaits. Do not be provincial in your spiritual world.

I have called My Body to an anointing of carrying out "greater works" to "turn the world upside down". And each of you, My sons and daughters, are a vital part of that call. Come and share your light—"give and it will be given back to you."

Live for the power of Christ to manifest in you and let this be your reward.

> *These people have turned the world upside-down!*
> Acts 17:6

My Call—A Treasure

Your surrender to Me involves a full commitment. There is no holding back, no control from you, no personally based expectations. When I call you, I call all of you.

A surrendered life brings Heavenly peace, but is more than likely going to present earthly consternation. For what I promise you is Me.

Your ability or willingness to surrender is an indicator of your relationship to Me. Will you trust Me? Have you received My love enough to know just how much I care for your every breath?

My Spirit is with you, leading you to surrender. It is why I ask you to die daily (Luke 9:23) because it puts you in a posture to give up freely what you rightfully deem your own. But remember, you are merely the steward of what I bestow. I seek your active part in the Kingdom life for this earth.

As a soldier of Christ, await, expect your next directive from Me. Do not discern the earthly merits of My leading for how much comfort or pleasure it might bring.

For My leading is sure to take you from your comfort zone, but, I promise, into a deeper, more fulfilling connection to Me and how I desire your life to look. What will it be for you? "Decide this day whom you will serve." (Joshua 24:15) My peace transcends earthly discomfort.

My call is a treasure to be sought, not a burden to be shunned.

I will give you everything you need to carry out My work in your life, the life I have given to you, a life that portrays My eternal love.

> *If anyone would come after me,*
> *he must deny himself and take up his cross daily*
> *and follow me.*
> *Luke 9:23*

My Presence Invades Your Every Prayer

Don't underestimate Me. If you believe I am God and you know what I'm capable of, and you know that I live in you, the Christian life should ever hold anticipation that I am ready to move mightily at any moment.

The issue for many is when. I want you to have an abiding presence with Me at all times so that "when?" is not an issue. Live as if each time you invoke My power—in intercession, sharing My message, loving each other—you expect Me to act.

Often, the larger matter is "are you listening to Me when I say it's time to act?" I do not work around your schedule. Your life is not your own; you are mine. And I am yours—yours to love, cry out to, invoke, praise, exalt, share, enjoy.

I am with you in everything, but do you always take time to see Me? Linger awhile with Me. Look for Me in the "smaller" things as well as what you deem greater. There is nothing insignificant that I am a part of, for "great is the glory of the Lord."

As "deep calls unto deep," I speak to the depth of any situation where I am invoked. I am working in your every call to Me, wanting to draw you closer, if only you'll recognize Me.

Like a waterfall whose roar you grow accustomed to and no longer take notice, My voice calls forth. Do not "get used to" Me.

I am never routine, predictable, or dull. Those are of the world and you, My friends, are only passing through.

Stay diligent to hear My plea. Focus on My goodness and abundant grace.

Never forget My awesome presence never fades, but invades your every prayer and makes possible the miraculous.

> *Deep calls to deep in the roar of your waterfalls;*
> *all your waves and breakers*
> *have swept over me.*
> *Psalm 42:7*

The Infinite Now

Come, feast on My daily bread. I have an abundance of grace each day available for you to take in and see Me within it. Come and be with Me in the present moment.

Do not savor for long the old for I am always doing a new and greater thing with you. Like manna, some want to hold on to the present favor, but why, when I have an infinite supply of grace for you? Some fear the good will fade away and there will be nothing new. Others never seek what is right before them today and continually yearn for a new tomorrow that never comes.

I am in eternity, without a past or future, but you experience it only a moment at a time. I see it all. What you see now is only part of a much greater whole of who I am. Trust Me that I am in your past, present, and future in a way that you cannot perceive. But your greatest experience of Me is now. Don't miss Me.

My present grace is ever revealing of Me so do take time today to bask in My presence. Do not get lost in past glory or future unknowns. I am gloriously with you always, but there is no time like the present to seek My face. How will you see Me today, right now, if you are not diligently present with Me, but lost in the past or future? Seek Me—today—and you will find Me.

Knock and the door will be opened to you.
Matthew 7:7

Abundance

To the extent that you will surrender control of your life to Me will you find a deeper sense of contentment in My promise to care for you and supply every need.

"I have come that you may have life more abundantly." (John 10:10).

This involves your submission to let go into Me. You are not leading; you are being led.

As your will and mine come together, you will see more of the promised life I have called you to. This is My will for you: abundance. Put no faith in your dying flesh, your finite thought patterns, your limited vision.

How can I plead with you more to let you know how deeply My desire for you is a fruitful life? Examine your mindset—is it surrendered fully to Me? Are there automatic thought patterns that lock Me out? Is your perspective one of faith-filled joy?

Let go whatever is not of Me and that which does not line up with My Word. I have your victory—it awaits those bold enough to stand for it and see the power of My will.

*This is to my Father's glory,
that you bear much fruit,
showing yourselves to be my disciples.
John 15:8*

MY PRESENCE IN AN ACTIVE DAY

Come into My heart and seek daily direction.

Each event of your day is meant to be an extension of prayer to Me. How much of your life has simply become tasks to be done or endured while joy is lacking altogether?

I am with you and in everything you do.

It is your choice, your will, that invokes My presence in a deeper way. Have you truly spent time with Me to know how it is I am seeking to include your works into My glory?

Yours is a life created for joy and peace, even amidst trials and the seemingly mundane.

As you grasp how much My presence goes before you and remains with you in all you do and experience, you'll begin to realize how vital a role you play. Do not lose focus of Me throughout your active day.

I am your source for joy, hope, light and you are My source to bring this message of the living gospel to a weary world. Don't miss out on these opportunities for bringing My presence forth.

*Surely you have granted him eternal blessings
and made him glad with the joy of your presence.
Psalm 21:6*

AWESOME CHANGE

Your faith and your trust are in Me, not in the fulfillment of any one of your desires. Be strong in your faith and trust by constantly building your spirit with praise, prayer, thanksgiving. You never fully know how I will manifest answered prayer. It always involves a process, one that ultimately brings you closer to Me. You may have want of a wish or desire: I have in mind an even greater result.

So often this result comes via the cross and a further dying to self which seldom looks or feels promising to you. Instead, you often cry out to be removed from any pain while I am in the midst of taking you through the fire of refinement. When you go through this and reach the other side, not only will you see Me with you, but you will grow in character and holiness. There is really no other easier way.

Stay focused then on Me and My ways for building you and answering your prayer. Surrender yourself along with your request and let Me be the developer of a multi-faceted, awesome change. I know the deeper, eternal picture and will always bring about what is best for you.

My only motivation is My wondrous, abiding love for you. Remember My love as you struggle, for I am taking you to a much greater place than you were.

Go in peace. Your journey has the Lord's approval.
Judges 18:6

Burning Constant

Be diligent in your search for Me. Never take for granted the awesome opportunity you have at any moment to enter into My presence. The devil seeks to destroy this beautiful fellowship continually. He is a formidable foe whenever you are not regularly in the Spirit.

He will try to tempt you toward lukewarm waters where you can deceive yourself into believing you are diligently drawing on more of Me, when, in fact, you have gradually slipped into a perilously cold place open to attacks of the enemy. Do not be deceived.

Do not wait for your next problem to seek Me in a deeper way then slip back into an earthly comfort zone of your own creation. It will cause a wavering in your heart that will lead to dissatisfaction.

Instead, keep your passion for Me burning constant. You never know where the devil lurks unless you stay with the One who knows his schemes against you. At any time you may find yourself surrounded by the darkness, be it sudden or gradual. Will you be in a position to resist and find your freedom?

One sure way to stay ahead of the devil's plan is to stay close to Me, your Lord, your Savior. He was defeated at the cross and remains a defeated foe. Though the devil may tempt and torment, he has no victory over the committed believer who will stand with Me using the power of the Holy Spirit to keep him down.

Of course, I have no fear of the devil—nor should you.

Obey My commands. Seek My guidance. Answer My call.

Come, walk with Me daily and I will be "a lamp to your feet, and a light to your path." (Psalm 119:105)

Be self-controlled and alert. Your enemy the devil prowls around like a roaring lion looking for someone to devour. Resist him, standing firm in the faith.

I Peter 5:8-9

THE HOLY VISION

Your life demands an over-arching vision of My purpose for your existence. It is too easy to lose your way amidst the day-to-day challenges. And it is too easy to forget I am your Adonai, your Lord, your Savior.

Let your earthly vision reflect My heavenly one and color it with songs of praise, declarations of My truth, the flags of spiritual warfare, and just being present to Me on a regular basis.

Too often, I hear, "Why?", "When?", "How?", "Me?" I have already and am continually speaking to you the answers for this life.

As you seek My view of your life, like scattered pieces of a puzzle, it will come together in a more meaningful whole. It is not for you to lament what you haven't done or how you can never see what I could possibly do through you. No, your job is that of surrender. Then My vision will shine brightly in ways you've never seen.

You need a heavenly, holy vision to guide, sustain, encourage, and lead for your everyday journey. Without it—who are you?

Why do you do what you do in the way that you do it? Is it just reaction to what the world dictates? Or is your life a living testament to the person of the Holy Spirit, alive and manifesting in you?

Come and see My light.

The vision I see for you is one of joy, hope, purpose and it brings us closer together. It is not without its earthly trials, but it is linked to your eternal sonship in the Kingdom of God.

And that vision, My child, is far greater than you'll know in this short lifetime.

Pray to keep it ever before you and it will keep you forever in My peace.

> *Where there is no vision, the people perish.*
> *Proverbs 29:18*

ACTUAL IDENTITY

With whom or what is your identity attached? It is a daily challenge to keep your heart focused on the source of all that you are—your loving, heavenly Father.

Is there a job, a person, a role to which you relate that you see as your source which "defines" you? Do you tend toward those areas of personal strengths or what you desire to help you identify how you see yourself and what you portray to the world?

Virtually every identity you hold on to is fleeting, but for the one you have in Me. The more you cling to them, the more unstable you'll feel, the more like the world you'll become.

Your talents and abilities, family and friends, jobs and ministries are gifts. At best, pray that you are a good steward of them and be grateful for each day you continue to have them by My grace. And it is My will that provides and sustains all your gifts, including life itself.

One day in Heaven, your existence will consist of none of what you know now outside of our relationship.

In this will you find your actual identity, for it began even before you came to earth and it will remain in eternity.

Your life is hidden with Christ in God.
Colossians 3:3

My Heart Moves My Hand

I am calling you to be intimately present to Me.

I come running to you when you reach to touch Me.

I so long to impart a touch of My heart to you for My love for you cannot be contained.

Words fail the true expression of how much I long to embrace you and hold you near.

Look always to My heart filled with tender love for you, for it is My heart that moves My hand.

Look away from the difficulties that surround you. It is in and through these I am working, shaping you towards a more perfect love, one that will allow you to draw more deeply into My eternal love.

God is able to make all favor abound to you.
2 Corinthians 9:8.

GOD LOVE

What kind of love dies on a cross for a world that earned destruction?

This is a heavenly love that defies human experience, one that you are unlikely to see outside of a Godly realm.

The cross of Christ shows the world how God loves and is able to forgive as part of that love. Nothing else can offer this kind of giving, loving acceptance.

Many of My people see it and think they could never love their enemy like that. Yet, I have placed My Holy Spirit inside each of you with the capability of honoring your fellow man with this very love.

It is more a battle for your will than your heart, for I have already made you a new creation. (II Corinthians 5:17)

The rest is up to you: how much of this Godly love will you accept and, in turn, give away?

You will need a cross when you choose to love My way for no flesh can act without the bondage of self-seeking.

And for most of the time, your sacrifice of love is minimal, typically needing only a small step to deny yourself. On occasions, you will be asked to bear a heavier cross of love. Whenever and whatever situation arises, I am there with you and in you to reflect My life.

It is not an easy way, but it is the only way. It is My love and the world best sees it when you live it.

Let the love of Christ in you flow from your personal cross that chooses neighbor over self and sees the greater reward of living a life pleasing to Me.

> *Therefore, if anyone is in Christ, he is a new creation;*
> *the old has gone, the new has come!*
> *II Corinthians 5:17*

Relying on Me

Your dependence on Me is something I spend a lifetime, often, waiting for you to give to Me.

It is an essential element of a life of faith, yet you yearn to stay in control for what you see as an easier path. But it is not.

Your life is constantly beset by challenges and attacks from the enemy of your soul. The devil is ever inviting you to unfurl a banner of fear, pride, lust, bitterness, self-pity that will shut out the light of Godly love, further pulling you into deeper despair.

These arrows of the enemy are easily defeated in surrendering them to My power. And best defeated early in the thought stage.

You are challenged with numerous thoughts every hour of every day, each requiring a decision and a discernment from you. Which way will you give in to? The way of righteousness? Or the way of bondage?

You will never be strong enough to consistently choose righteousness without a full dependence on the Holy Spirit.

You face a relentless foe seeking a cunning compromise, who has worked his evil since human beings first appeared. And without a full surrender to your Lord and Savior, the devil will succeed. (Philippians 2:21 "For all seek their own, not the things which are of Christ".)

Rely fully on the power of the Word of the Spirit to crush the enemy's plans. Keep on relying on it.

Implant it in your heart and head. Because the enemy will not quit, do not let go of Me.

Dependence means a full surrender, leaning your full weight on Me constantly. As you depend on Me for your next breath, so, too, keep Me ever in your focus. I am your daily bread, "the peace that surpasses all understanding" (Philippians 4:7), the one in whom you "have your being". (Acts 17:28)

I love you too much to ever let you go. Let Me take the offensive against the devil and I will show you My victory. Even when, or especially when, you feel defeated and weary. Surrender to the Risen Lord.

Arise, shine; for your light has come!
And the glory of the Lord is risen upon you.
Isaiah 60:1

The Voice of Deeper Freedom

Where is your heart today? Is it settled with Christ your Savior? Or is it being pulled and drawn in a direction that is taking you further from the sound of My voice?

In order to be willing and ready to obey Me, you must first have a heart that is fully connected to My will. Your objections and impediments may be subtle beyond where you recognize them as interference between us.

But My only condition is and always has been a totally committed life seeking My will alone. Does that describe you? Can you hear My voice? And when you hear it, are you ready to act on it right away? Or does the world still hold some better promise that warrants you to do things your own way?

The free will you have is a gift. As you exercise it toward reaching Me, you are using it as I have intended. Every choice or movement of your will to Me is an act of love toward Me. And it brings you a deeper, abiding freedom to be like Christ.

Jesus' life was the ultimate continual submission to the Father. Yet there was no one more free to love and to serve than the Savior.

You, My children, can know this freedom also—the freedom of a submitted heart. Let go of your worldly expectations, personal fulfillments, and gratifications of the flesh.

Where are they taking you? If not toward Me, then let them go. Keep your heart enfolded in mine and see yourself living a Christ-life.

Lord, you have heard the desire of the humble; you will prepare their heart; you will cause your ear to hear.
Psalm 10:17

GREATER CAPACITY FOR LOVE

Wherever you may find yourself today—rejoice! Let him who redeems your life have his way in you, for the course I have set only leads to the deeper truth of who I am.

Bear up under the strain of life's burdens and look to Me for your strength.

A dependent you is a holier you. Do not let bitterness seep in—My love and desires for you are too great to ever believe I do not have your ultimate interests in My heart.

The misguided attitudes and ideas of this world will seek constantly to enlist your approval.

My truth is eternal and has withstood centuries of worldly pressure, always prevailing.

This should comfort you during ever-changing times when what is "certain" today will soon change.

Faithfulness to Me and My ways will always serve you and the body of Christ best, regardless of outward appearances.

My truth comes from the Holy Spirit within you and allows you discernment beyond limited, temporal thinking. Never underestimate that truth and the power it offers.

The Spirit you hold within you has the capacity to enact radical changes when you align it with Kingdom purpose.

But trust that this purpose, My purpose, is good.

It may not always gratify the flesh, but when it's from Me, it will lead you toward the abundant life I have promised.

> *Seek his face always.*
> Psalm 105:4

MIRACLE LOVE-WORKING POWER

My abundance is evident in My people. I have called you to be a direct source of My grace and Heavenly power.

My Holy Spirit lives inside you—what is it you cannot do in My name?

The story of Acts lives on in you. And I long to take the Body to greater heights of miracle love-working power.

Take My love with you and see what awesome things we can do. You never truly know how I will manifest until you shed My light into your life. Be willing to step up and step out for the sake of My Kingdom.

So great a price has been paid for you—you have value beyond what you can imagine. I would not entrust My precious nature to anyone unless they were worthy of it. The blood of the Lamb has made you worthy, righteous, and able to carry out great works.

Rejoice in this: that I have called you My own. This is your inheritance of the Father. Receive it. Share it. Live it. Let the world know that I am a living God, relevant everyday, and ever longing to live in and through you.

*You may ask Me for anything
in My name and I will do it.
John 14:12-14*

MY ALL FOR YOU

Enter in.

Come, giving fully of yourself to Me. When I call you, I seek all of you, lest you grow lukewarm (Revelation 3:16) and be good for little or nothing.

I have given My all for you and expect the same, in your worship, your prayer, your fellowship, your ministry to the Body, your receiving of all good gifts from above.

How can you do anything in My name unless you are spiritually alive, watching, waiting actively, expecting, listening, hoping, stepping out?

For the kingdom of God is not a matter of talk but of power.
I Corinthians 4:20

ENJOYING TIME IN MY PRESENCE

"Could you not watch with Me one hour?" (Matthew 26:40)

I am seeking your heart again. For I am reaching to you from My heart, a heart of infinite love.

You can reach back to Me in prayer. But how are you doing that? Is it a struggle to find time to be with Me? I want you to stay "fresh," always filled with what I most want for you.

Each day brings a new indwelling part of My Spirit and it's yours for the taking.

You need My light to penetrate the darkness of uncertainty, fear, and doubt that daily visits you. Never be in a position of making decisions based on worry or earthly persuasions of the soul.

As you stay close to Me through prayer, you will hear My voice.

I have promised that I will lead you, direct you, and answer you. If you doubt, it is your self-doubt leading you astray. When you fear deeply, are you really trusting Me?

You have needs. I have provision.

I am not looking for all of your time, but in the time you choose to give, I do want all of you. I go wherever your prayer goes: to fill your heart when you praise, to touch the lives of those you pray for, and to speak to your spirit when we commune.

I can never have enough of you.

Do you ever have enough of Me? I have created you as an eternal being because it will take eternity for you to begin to grasp how much love I have for you.

Spending time wisely in My presence will give you a taste of My eternal glory and help to make your Christian life the awesome life that I have intended it to be.

He will take great delight in you.
Zephaniah 3:17

Forgiveness

Let your forgiveness be complete.

Hold back nothing to the so-called "undeserving." This is grace in action, your opportunity to emulate the divine. Your flesh will reap little satisfaction with this simple act, but your spirit will be free.

Forgiveness is not a choice; it is a command. It is so essential to your living a glorious life that you must never ponder your action to forgive.

Decide ahead of the next offense you will undoubtedly experience. And decide right now to forgive. Let justice and mercy triumph in a Godly way by your letting go. "It is for freedom that I have set you free." (Galatians 5:1)

A true measure of your being Christ-like is in your readiness to forgive others at all times.

Be generous and thorough in your mercy, just as you received forgiveness from the Father. Nothing will so hinder your walk with Me than unrepented sin and forgiveness held back. Just imagine if Jesus held back his forgiving the way you often do? Where would you be as a result?

I am your source of ever deepening love. Your quest for revenge or passive-aggressive coldness towards those who have wronged you will never do anything for our relationship. Until you let go.

Come, walk in My freedom today and everyday. I have given you the gift of reconciliation to keep you free to love one another and to be free to always walk in My light.

If you love those who love you, what reward will you get?
Matthew 5:46

THE AUTHENTIC FOLLOWER

Come near to Me—let Me see the real you, free and unfettered from what you think you are. It is easy for you to hide the true person I created you to be behind so much worldly culture.

I am seeking the authentic follower, one who lives out of My love rather than in doing those things you somehow deem you are supposed to do. Has your repentance cut to the heart with your most burning desire to stay intimately connected to Me? When you ask for My will to be in your life, are you prepared for all it could ask of you? My body is ever so often too practical in what they call faith.

The world you live in provides more assurance than perhaps you should be relying upon as a follower of Christ. Where does your abandonment for this world begin and your utter dependence on Me take hold? In every area: finances, relationships, loving your enemies, witnessing My love, deep and lasting repentance, careers, interceding for "hopeless" causes, building up the body—what else? Can you hear Me?

I "have blessed you with every spiritual blessing in the heavenly places in Christ." (Ephesians 1:3)

You have been blessed and grace-filled to live an abundant life (John 10:10), one of victory, hope, joy—because you have a Lord and a Savior.

I have availed to you Holy Spirit fire from Heaven to touch you, for you to touch others in My name.

Don't miss Me in favor of a more comfortable routine of daily living. Yours is the Jericho road, the one Jesus followed to the cross. Are you taking up your daily cross to follow Me? (Luke 9:23) So often this walk comes in the simple daily choices you make for Me— or don't make.

Will you live for Me today? How?

Will you forgive that offending brother or sister?

Will you pray for your lost enemy?

Will you praise Me like David did, free of the care of others?

Will you accept the gifts I offer through the Holy Spirit and use them to exalt others?

Will you trust Me when I call you on to the water?

This gift of the life of Christ you have been given is far too short to let it pass by. Give Me all of you. I will receive you in love and use whatever you give Me for My glory.

Consider the worth your life has to Me.

But to each one of us
grace was given according to the measure of Christ's gift.
Ephesians 4:7

THE PARAMOUNT RELATIONSHIP

All I do and all that occurs in your life—whatever happens to you—it is all for the building of our relationship.

I have purpose for you beyond the life you know. What happens here all points to Me.

Do you, too, see our relationship as paramount to all other things? Or do you get lost in the temporal "importance" of life as you know it? Any achievement you know is lacking if you do not have Me at the core of it. Is your job, your home, your income, where you live as important as truly knowing Me? I see My earthly gifts and provisions as a means to the even greater gift of a deeper relationship. Remember to "Seek first the Kingdom of God and its righteousness and all these things will be added unto you." (Matthew 6:33) "For what is your life? It is even a vapor that appears for a little time and then vanishes away." (James 4:14)

I urge you to make the most of your time. I will love you and support all earthly endeavors that are of My will. Beyond that, you are only striving in vain for a poor substitute for Me, something which will only lead you further from Me and down a sinful path.

Wake up and declare what really matters to you—or what really should matter. That is your God, My Spirit flowing in and through you. "For with you is the fountain of life…" (Psalm 36:9)

You will never find more joy, more fulfillment in anything else besides Me. Endure challenges as you have to, stand with Me when you feel alone, and know that I am calling you, drawing you home to My deepest love.

Do not miss out on this, the greatest thing your life will know.

Love the Lord your God with all your heart.
Matthew 22:37

THE FIRE OF MY GLORY

Forsake the unrighteous promise of the world's comfort, for it is short-lived and stands on shaky ground. A quick fix or temporal route to happiness, or at least the avoidance of despair, will only take you deeper into the dark. Perhaps you have become addicted to worldly ways—and you are completely unaware. Lasting peace and true joy can only come from the eternal love of your heavenly Father.

I am what you long for, all you need. But I don't come to you by your ways or limited desires. My truth is the only truth and you know "My ways are not your ways." (Isaiah 55:8) My peace is not based on circumstances; My joy is not ephemeral happiness.

I am much greater than the best this world has to offer. Where My presence is brought in, despair becomes hope; bondage, freedom; the ordinary, spectacular; fear becomes boldness; death becomes life. Yes, I work in the natural, but I bring supernatural grace to the most unlikely of situations.

My Spirit offers access to this unlimited favor, based on My desirous love for you. Do not let your devotion to Me become like an addictive fix that seeks only partial relief.

And do not let your shortcomings, or sin, or lack of belief, your fears, worries, or lost hope be a hindrance to seeking My miracle working power; for it is working amidst My ever-present, deepest love for your good will.

And amidst days of suffering and discomfort, go beyond where you are, what you're doing, who you've become, and, again, step into this "grace in which you stand"—already—and to which you "have access". By faith.

Dare to believe I am your God, capable of anything. Seek My heart and My hand will follow. By faith.

Dare to trust Me—"In all your ways, acknowledge Me." (Proverbs 3:6) I am just beyond your circumstance with all the power and the fire of My glory ready to envelop you. Let go of your finite solutions and welcome in the King of Glory.

We rejoice in the hope of the glory of God.
Romans 5:1-3

MY KINGDOM WORLD

The veil that is the world, as you see it and experience it, does not, in any way, diminish who I am or how I act in and upon it.

Though not fully revealed, My glory is as abundant where you are now as where I stand eternally.

I am unfolding My Kingdom power to you whenever you reach toward Me in prayer, praise, submission, desire.

In fact, this supernatural Kingdom is essentially more real, more alive, and certainly more powerful than what is not eternal. Therefore I call you to My Kingdom world.

It is best known through faith and experienced in My presence.

For here is your home. You are now on mission to bring My light and truth, My resurrection power to My created world.

Do not let a dim world view jade your image of who I really am. I am well beyond the created and always exceed your greatest thoughts.

I am beyond containment, but not beyond direction, that is, where you direct Me in prayer. I will go where prayer goes if you'll take Me there.

My Heavenly Kingdom is so much closer than you could realize. It is not distant nor long in coming.

It is among you and goes forth in My Word and worship.

Beyond your limited senses, take hold of what I offer and witness My revelation.

> *It has not yet been revealed what we shall be.*
> *I John 3:2*

SURPASSING THOUGHT

I am greater than your thoughts—your thoughts of Me, of the future, of your present situation, as well as of others and those of yourself.

For what are your thoughts and where do they come from? Are they fully in submission to Godly authority? How often are your thoughts the product of past hurts, remembered sins, perceived inadequacies, fear of unknowns, and so much more that is not from the Lord?

Yet, your thoughts typically rule you.

Even the best of your mind images are but short-lived and not nearly enough to sustain a meaningful action.

And do not your thoughts affect how you feel, and, as you let them, your motivation? Where does this leave you for Kingdom living? Are your thoughts and feelings tempting you to think less of the power of God?

Your thoughts are very small compared to the majesty that is—truly is—God Jehovah, your Creator, Redeemer, Lover, Healer, Helper, and Friend.

"The just shall live by faith." (Habakkuk 2:4) My faith to you is a gift allowing you to transcend your present darkness to move into My realm of truth, where hope, deliverance, joy, and victory reign.

Take hold of this faith. It is what made men and women in the scriptures live amazing lives. It is what takes you beyond suffering, lost hope, fears, defeat, and into the exceedingly abundant life I promised. (Ephesians 3:20)

"Therefore it is of faith that it might be according to grace, so that the promise might be sure to all…" (Romans 4:16)

Your faith in Me is real and will take you beyond your transient thought life, which can be so easily corrupted.

I am always above your thoughts and moving in ways that you could never know or perceive in the intellect.

Only know that My heart is with you always and ever moving you towards My glory. I can and I will.

Trust Me.

How precious to me are your thoughts God!
Psalm 139:17

AN AMAZING TODAY

Your future lies in how you're handling your present in Me. There is truly no time for you except the present, here and now.

It is in that moment of your being that connects with Me right now that is the height of our relationship. And it's all you're guaranteed. (James 4:13-14)

What I ask you to do now has direct impact on your tomorrow—don't miss it.

And do not wait for a future time to act. If you do all that I show you today, you will be prepared for that day I already see ahead. I am in your future—trust that I know how to get you there.

My people get so overly concerned about a future of their own imagination that they lose heart today and begin planting the seeds of defeat. "Therefore do not worry about tomorrow, for tomorrow will worry about itself. Each day has enough trouble of its own." (Matthew 6:34)

The enemy desires to take you in your mind to two places: your unchanging past and your uncertain future. But I have redeemed your past and promised your future. (Jeremiah 29:11)

Do pray for what is to come, but not on your own terms. Any effective prayer involves surrender, leaving Me free to exercise My will for your life. Then, I will begin to unfold My plan and make straight the paths before you. (Hebrews 12:13)

I see your life together as one; there is no past or future from God's eternal perspective.

Free yourself from time-bound fears and worries. Focus on Me—right now.

I know just what you need at this moment as to how it will relate to and what you need for your future.

You will find tremendous peace in the present with Me.

Obeying My will—not man-made circumstances—each day will mold you into the spiritual person I created you to be. (Psalm 119:133-134)

Let My hand take you toward an amazing tomorrow by seeking My loving heart today.

The Lord is a rewarder of those who diligently seek him.
Hebrews 11:6

Focal Point

Don't lose track of My heart in seeking your answered prayer.

Seek My heart foremost and My hand will follow.

I am your focus, your focal point—not your disturbing circumstances. I am Jehovah Jireh, your Provider.

Draw nearer to Me—that is where you'll find your joy.

I will make things happen for you—your works are minimally important to the true answer. Rather, seek the One who gives you all the answers.

Your trials are meant to draw you to Me—don't miss the opportunity.

Are you so foolish? After beginning with the Spirit,
are you now trying to attain your goal by human effort?
Galatians 3:3

THE VOICE OF TRUTH

The world so easily entangles you with its lies, menial thinking, negativity, fears, and doubts. These creep into your soul and jade the way you approach life, especially the way you approach Me.

I am continually speaking My heart to you, but against the backdrop of worldly dross, My voice is faint, or, if heard, becomes so contrary to what you've been exposed to that it can easily be dismissed as folly.

Come away from the world. (Romans 12:2) Cleanse your spirit, soul, and body of the build-up of the things of this world. "Blessed are the pure in heart, for they shall see God." (Matthew 5:8)

As you deny your flesh, repent, and let go of worldly thought, you will hear the voice of the Holy Spirit more clearly. It is likely to be contrary to what you've been hearing around you, mainly because it is the voice of truth that cannot be denied.

And it brings with it life. Prepare your heart and mind with praise and prayer to receive My Word. It is victory and will bring comfort and the "peace which surpasses all understanding." (Philippians 4:7)

Listen to his voice, and hold fast to him,
for the Lord is your life.
Deuteronomy 30:20

GODLY TALENT

I will be strength for your weakness, but what about your strengths or talents?

Can you be weak in your perceived strengths enough to allow My power to make your works greater? What would that take? A lot of humility and surrender.

It is too easy to play to your strengths to the point where you can unconsciously be much less dependent on Me. Is that, then, really a good thing?

The talents I give are not meant to be independent of Me for they still come from Me. "Every good and perfect gift is from above, coming down from the Father of the heavenly lights, who does not change like shifting shadows." (James 1:17)

Personal strengths tend to give a measure of control or mastery to your life that you were never meant to have. When these are threatened—why is it you feel out of control? The situation is not out of control—it's in My hands. You are now, literally, out of control.

Does it ever occur to you that My loosening your grip on a situation you have long controlled is My way of "fixing" it for you? Isn't that an answer to yours or somebody's prayer—that I would intervene? How can I if you've willed it shut?

You, My child, are merely the steward of My gifts and situations. Don't let your times of prosperity delude you into thinking otherwise.

Godly stewardship always involves full surrender at any time for no reason other than My wisdom.

And My love.

Consider it blessing when I take control of your "control". I am deeply present in your weakness in a way that I'm not as much in your perceived strengths.

> *My power is made perfect in weakness.*
> *II Corinthians 12:9*

Looking Out For You

Are you spending too much time thinking in your prayer?

True communion with Me is more about abandoning your own thoughts and bringing your body, mind, and spirit willfully under submission to Me. Unsubmitted thoughts can entangle you and keep your will in control.

Does your prayer time bring you freedom and release you to joy? Or does it create deeper worry and concern?

Prepare your heart as you come to Me, knowing that I am a loving God who awaits your plea. "For he who comes to God must believe that he is, and that he is a rewarder of those who diligently seek him." (Hebrews 11:6)

Like the father of the prodigal (Luke 15), I am looking out for you, expecting your arrival. And once I see you, I will come running to you, My beloved. Trust that I am your God.

Trust Me to be your God. Let our time of communing be one that brings light to your darkness, joy to your heart, hope for your journey.

I am looking for you to lead in with your spirit.

Let your soul be refreshed; walk away with renewed vision into the life of victory I have called you toward.

Whatever your trials, you can still rejoice and find joy in My presence. Know that I walk before you and beside you at all times.

Your thoughts are incomplete glimpses of the true spiritual, heavenly life and need constant submission to prayer. Let Me be your guide and I will sustain in you My clear vision for truth and life.

> *You will fill me with joy in your presence,*
> *with eternal pleasures at your right hand.*
> Psalm 16:11

Surrendering Strain

I exhort you to stand firmly in your faith in Me as trials surround you. If you do not, you are no better off than an unbeliever, tossed about by your worries, fears, and negative imagination.

It is essentially your choice. I have blessed you with every spiritual blessing (Ephesians 1:3) and equipped you with My inner power to withstand the onslaught of a lying enemy. (Ephesians 6:10-18)

The battles of the Christian life are many. Unless you "take up my yoke" (Matthew 11:29) constantly, your life will become an onerous one filled with stress and strain. And what fruit will that bear? You will become so focused on your troubles that My face will begin to fade as, inwardly, you strive to work out your worries and begin to demand relief from Me, rather than bear up under the strain toward deeper spiritual growth.

I am with you in your difficult times. I am not always a "feel good" God. True joy comes in knowing Me and surrendering your life, your will, to the one who truly loves and cares for you.

Let go of whatever it is that is keeping you down.

Experience the freedom of a life lived in and through Me.

> *By this gospel you are saved.*
> *I Corinthians 15:2*

GREATER ANSWERS

Yes, I am with you—always. From the moment your heart first made intention to seek Me, I came running to you. I hear your prayers and act immediately toward them. But in My way, and in My time. My purposes reach much further than the granting of your concrete desires. I seek to make you holy, to let the Christ in you shine ever brighter. Is that your hope also, whenever you seek My help? Is your petition a surrender? Or a command?

I see your life in its eternal context and know exactly how to respond to your prayer. Trust that I will do so. Let your will align with mine. Know that your petitions are continuously before Me and I am working out even greater answers than what your limited scope could ever have asked for. My response to your heartfelt prayer comes about because of My love, My compassion for you. "In the day when I cried out, You answered me, And made me bold with strength in my soul." (Psalm 138:3)

I never delay in answering your prayer. Do not confuse what you believe the answer should be versus what I know is best for you and what will ultimately deepen our relationship.

Fear not, for I am with you;
Be not dismayed, for I am your God. I will strengthen you
Yes, I will help you
I will uphold you with My righteous right hand.
Isaiah 41:10

THE ATMOSPHERE OF HEAVEN

Rejoice! For today there is rejoicing in Heaven. God's glory fills the air, unencumbered by earthly fears and concerns. This is your future dwelling place. Yet the glory of God fills the earth, too. (Psalm 19:1)

Are you allowing it to bring you joy regardless of your circumstance? How is it that God and his Heaven are so full of joy always when all around there appears trouble? What is it that allows God's rejoicing amidst so many apparent trials?

The freedom of an eternal perspective, knowing you are victorious always in Jesus Christ. It is the things that are passing and fleeting that cause such unhappiness and turmoil. "So we fix our eyes not on what is seen, but on what is unseen. For what is seen is temporary, but what is unseen is eternal." (II Corinthians 4:18)

Even your best times are only short-lived and not enough to keep you truly joyful. It is only in Me, your faithful savior and redeemer where you will find truthful joy, that which has an everlasting foundation.

For in Me is your hope, your joy, your strength. I rejoice in you because I made you and I know who you are and why you are on earth. "For I know the plans I have for you," declares the Lord, "plans to prosper you and not to harm you, plans to give you hope and a future." (Jeremiah 29:11)

And all I do is for My glory and your greater good, to draw you nearer to Me.

And in that, I always rejoice. Beyond your circumstances. Beyond what is seen.

> *My spirit rejoices in God my Savior.*
> *Luke 1:47*

Believing for the Unbelievable

How "big" is your God today?

Is the living Lord a vital presence for you or just another something amidst your busy life? Does your relationship with Me build your faith in who I am, enough that you can begin to believe for the unbelievable? Or am I a "safe" God, easily contained within the limits of your temporal world?

I long to manifest My awesome and amazing presence in the world.

At times, this can come across in instantaneous, miraculous outpourings evident to all. At others, it is a gradual, steady flow of divine power that transforms in time, but carries My equally powerful grace with it.

Be filled continually with My Spirit (Ephesians 5:18) and see Me for who I really am—your all-loving, all-powerful, life-changing God.

My glory does not fade or diminish with your mood or lack of attention toward Me.

The same God who created Heaven and earth stands with you today. Receive Me.

Then give Me away: in prayer, in fellowship.

Revere Me: in praise, in worship, in thanksgiving.

Look around you and see My manifestation in My creation "For since the creation of the world God's invisible qualities—his eternal power and divine nature—have been clearly seen, being understood from what has been made, so that men are without excuse." (Romans 1:20)

I am yours.

Invite Me in on every occasion and see My glorious presence living in and through you.

Christ is the same yesterday, today, and forever.
Hebrews 13:8

An Undivided Self

Your divided loyalties will scatter you and lead your focus away from Me. Commit today to be single-minded for My Kingdom purposes.

The truth speaks only one language and is never to be questioned or compromised.

I have endowed you with the heavenly language to hear My voice in all matters right and wrong. Questioning, delaying, not seeking or listening will always lead you astray. And the further you drift from the eternal truth, the more difficult to discern anything else I speak to you hereafter.

Pray each day for an undivided heart—one that does not compromise My ways. One of the more effective schemes of the enemy is to divide—and then, conquer. No one part of a divided self is able to withstand the united front of satanic attack.

Counter with a united front of your own, whereby you choose to stay submitted to the loving, protective authority of the Holy Spirit. "For we have no power against this great multitude that is coming against us; nor do we know what to do, but our eyes are upon You." (II Chronicles 20:12)

An unwavering heart connected to Me is assured victory despite struggles and hardships.

Anything less will eventually lead you to a defeated life. Fear, impatience, revenge, idleness, entitlement can all feed the gradual division of your heart. Do not let these or other vices seep into your way of life, for they will only feed your flesh and devour your soul. "Hold firmly to the trustworthy message as it has been taught, so that you can encourage others by sound doctrine and refute those who oppose it." (Titus 1:9)

Give me an undivided heart that I may fear your name.
Psalm 86:11

SOMETHING AMAZING

Elevate your focus.

There is so much more to the spiritual life than what you typically see—or don't see. I am a God of order (I Corinthians 14:33) who is constantly orchestrating an infinite number of events that comprise your existence. And in this you play a large role, perhaps much greater than you realize. Never be lulled into the notion that nothing is occurring in your life.

I have equipped you with the greatness of My being. Therefore, you have a say in the workings not only of your world, but in the heavenly realms that impact your time and place.

Stay vigilant to your holiness, for it is through your holy vessel that I work from and translate to you My call on your life. You truly never know the next event that will befall you or a situation close to you. Is the way of holiness you walk in right now ready for what is coming at any moment?

If not, you could easily miss what I'm calling you toward. Or, you may find yourself unprepared and overwhelmed for what is happening once you are in the midst of it.

The devil is your sly enemy who gradually conditions you into an ordinary, complacent, compromising fool if you are not wise to his ways. (II Corinthians 2:11)

Do not let your busy routine take you away from Me.

In the same way that a diligent effort toward holiness through prayer, praise, and fellowship keeps you close to My Holy Spirit power and wisdom, a complacent, indolent, lacking desire to constantly seek Me will open the door to frequent sin without conviction and a mundane, powerless Christian life. At this point, are you much different than the non-believer? (James 1:14-16)

Take hold of the gifts I have chosen to share with you.

Never take them for granted and do not underestimate the power of the Holy Spirit that lives within your being.

Everyday it has something new to offer. Something amazing.

There is a small price to pay of your time and attention. But haven't you already sworn your whole life to Me?

Live like you have and see the awesome grace of your loving God pour out to you and through you.

For the grace of God that brings salvation has appeared to all.
Titus 2:11-14

An Experiential God

"Fear not, for I am with you; Be not dismayed, for I am your God. I will strengthen you, Yes, I will help you, I will uphold you with My righteous right hand." (Isaiah 41:10)

It is God who is able, not you alone. Even the slightest dependence on self will lead you away from Me. And this is neither difficult nor unlikely given natural human tendencies toward becoming too: busy, lazy, tired, complacent.

Too often, you may find yourself "spiritually malnourished" if you're steadily feeding on cursory prayer time; are overly indulged in worldly pursuits of work or leisure; or just become one-sided in your relationship with the Lord by taking his grace for granted. All of these inevitably lead back to self-reliance and feelings of inadequacy, spiritual fatigue, fear, and ultimately, vulnerability to the enemy.

I am an experiential God, meant to be lived and breathed at all times. (Acts 17:28)

How can I be God to you unless I am alive and active in your daily being?

My grace is there for the asking. I am with you always—won't you turn your face to Me?

In praise, I invade your heart with My presence. In teachings from My Word, you have My divine wisdom. In thanksgiving, I reveal to you the beauty and generosity of My incessant provision. In intercession, I let you move the hand of God to change impossible situations. In fellowship, you get a tangible expression of Me in one another. What could be more worthy of your time than these?

Your prayers are not just thoughts, wishes, dreams, aspirations, all the things you meant, but never took the heartfelt time, to express to Me.

I have called you to act in My name—"Ask, and it will be given to you; seek, and you will find; knock, and it will be opened to you; for everyone who asks receives, and he who seeks finds, and to him who knocks it will be opened." (Matthew 7:7-8) Consider the corollary: when you do not ask, seek, and knock, can you really expect to receive, find, and see openings?

Come home to the One who is able and eagerly willing to fill you to overflowing. You are My vessels, I am your God.

I have called you to live the extraordinary. Why settle for anything less?

"For in him we live and move and have our being."
As some of your own poets have said, "We are his offspring."
Acts 17:28

AMASS A STOREHOUSE

So much of this life in a spiritual sense is about dying. It is a daily, sometimes hourly event, but ironically vital to your life in Christ. "He who believes in Me, though he may die, he shall live." (John 11:25)

In the same way you mourn the final death of your lives, you mourn the daily passing of worldly ties even more.

You long to hold on to what you cannot have, nor what you really need. Yet each of you is merely passing through this world on the way to eternity. Why not let go of the temporal and amass a storehouse for the eternal? What is it you are holding on to that a dying to yourself would free you from?

Never confuse the means to a blessing with the source. Is it unforgiveness? Fleshly habits? Counterproductive relationships? An idol? Leave it on the altar and let the Lord bring new life to you. "Unless a grain of wheat falls into the ground and dies, it remains alone, but if it dies, it produces much grain." (John 12:24)

Whatever keeps you from coming closer to Me must go. It is the desires of your flesh that are called to die. But the promise of what I will resurrect from your willful dying to self is both eternally and immediately for your gain and My glory. "For if we died with him, we shall also live with him." (II Timothy 2:11)

The story of your life on earth is one of preparation for the next life, which will never end.

Your living unto Me is the key to freedom and peace right now: to enjoy the life I have called you to, not the one which you deem better, more interesting, or less difficult.

And it starts now, not at your funeral.

Die with Me now and you shall live the blessed life your spirit longs for and ready yourself to live with Me forever as My Kingdom heir.

*Now if we died with Christ,
we believe that we shall also live with him
Romans 6:8*

I WANT YOUR JOY

"These things I have spoken to you, that My joy may remain in you, and your joy may be full." (John 15:11)

Where on earth is your joy?

My heavenly Kingdom is unhindered, unending, delighting in Me eternally. Where is this fullness of joy for you today? Is it even attainable?

Left to your own devices, you will never find true, lasting joy. All the riches, relationships, knowledge, jobs, travel in and of themselves will leave you thirsting for more. Putting Me first, above all worldly goods, will reveal the goodness I want for you in any and all of these things.

And My joy is not limited to the pleasures of life. My presence brings you joy, peace, intimacy in the midst of life's ongoing trials. Your faith—trusting, knowing who I am to you—is the key to revealing My touch.

Do you know that I love you? And this life is built upon bringing you and Me closer. I will do so by whatever means possible. Though you experience suffering, I say, "Count it all joy." (James 1:2)

Finding joy amidst all your trials and challenges involves knowing Me—truly, deeply knowing Me—not knowing about Me, reciting "holy" words, or taking another's word for it.

I want you.

Know that we can have that kind of loving relationship, more intimate than any earthly one.

I will never disappoint, abandon, ignore, ridicule, or hurt you. I will bring to light My presence through every part of your life, every day. Look for Me.

Do not lose sight of My presence by getting caught up in personal happiness or worldly despair. The "path of life" is strewn with My presence and, with it, "fullness of joy".

Let your heavenly experience begin now.

In your presence is fullness of joy.
Psalm 16:11

MY POWER

Never underestimate the power of your Lord. I can reach any situation, person, place in any way, shape, or form I choose.

I am too often boxed-in by those who know Me, or claim to, and am often missed when I come knocking.

Let go of your preconceptions of My intervention.

> *I am the Lord, the God of all flesh:*
> *is there any thing too hard for me?*
> *Jeremiah 32:27*

MY NEXT MIRACLE

Prepare yourself for the unexpected, for My true grace is never what you've envisioned, lest it fall short of abundant provision. (John 10:10)

Your fears are neither as bad, nor is your hope as great as you imagine. This is all the more reason to submit them all to Me. Very often, the door to hope lies just beyond some of your greatest fears and the only pathway there is by trusting Me.

How will you know when a door of opportunity opens to you? Should you judge it by your limited experience, what you know, your limited abilities, or will you ever proceed? I have done mighty acts in visibly barren situations. Was it Moses' brilliance that gave him the leadership to guide My flock out of Egypt and to part the Red Sea? (Exodus 15) What kept the lions from devouring Daniel? (Daniel 6:21-23) Or the furnace flames from Shadrach, Meshach and Abednego? (Daniel 3:19-27) Did Paul suddenly change his mind from persecutor to evangelist? (Acts 9)

There is no precedent for My next miracle beyond that I AM. I am always doing a new thing and it will come like a wave over the land. Just stay in My flow and see the mighty hand of God, led by My generous love to redeem all.

I am doing a new thing!
Now it springs up; do you not perceive it?
Isaiah 43: 19

THE BEDROCK

I am your solid foundation upon which you can stand, no matter your situation. Should you feel the ground beneath you crumbling, check the foundation on which you stand. Is it Me? Or is it something of your own construction? (Matthew 7:27)

Many times you build your confidence on the success of the work I've called you to, not on the One who called you to do it.

And if it appears that you won't succeed, you may never attempt what I've called you to carry out. Whereas, when I am your source and strength, there is nothing to hold you back.

The broken ground beneath you is typically the topsoil of your personal confidence being washed away as the inevitable trials of life come at you.

Beneath it, however, stands the bedrock of My love, the all-sustaining grace that makes life possible. Let the loose dirt wash away. Build upon Me.

With Me as your foundation, you can take leaps of faith into unknown territory with more confidence than you've ever known. Belief in yourself need not be experiential or else you would seldom venture beyond your very small comfort zone.

What is it today that you doubt or fear? What's truly holding you back? Do you not recall that I will be with you wherever you go? (Matthew 28:20)

I never call where I don't provide, regardless of how challenging your responsibility appears.

I'm looking for commitment.

Are you "sold" on Me? Forever? Hot? Cold? Or lukewarm? (Revelation 3:15-16) How you act in a committed manner is much different than if you hold back.

I give you all of Me—I ask for all of you.

*Everyone who hears these words of mine
and does not put them into practice
is like a foolish man who built his house on sand.
Matthew 7:26*

I AM FOREVER

My Word and the truth it sets forth are eternally powerful. If you find yourself today under the bondage of your circumstances, measure what My Word says about you. Your troubles are passing. I am forever.

I have said you are victorious (Psalm 44:7), an overcomer (Luke 10:19), strong in the Lord (Exodus 15:2), anxious for nothing (Philippians 4:6), directed in your paths. (Proverbs 3:6)

These words have been tested and true for centuries and apply with equal power to you today. The devil's biggest lie is to have you believe otherwise. Regardless of what your actions, thoughts, and emotions drive you to believe about yourself, I see your finished work and I see Jesus in you.

Grab hold of this truth that lives within you and proclaim it boldly. Say what I say about you. The blood of the cross has forever redeemed you and is not dependent on your latest thoughts or feelings. The truth of My existence and real presence in your life trumps your best and worst circumstances. I bring My awesome presence into My Word, what it says, and wherever it is believed and proclaimed. Let My truth be the foundation of where you live each moment.

The truth shall set you free.
John 8:32

MAJESTY UNVEILED

You have far too much distress for one who claims to be walking in My presence.

I am a God who brings peace in the storm. (Psalm 107:28-30)

When the all-powerful, knowing, and loving God is with you at every moment, of what is it you are still afraid? Perhaps My majesty is blocked by soul-ish control. Is it fear? Upset of your creature comforts? Not enough focus on prayer and listening to the Spirit?

Where do you find yourself today? Am I truly Lord of your entire life? What will you do to return to Me?

I long to give you so much more if you'll let go of the fleeting, earthbound controls and trust that truly "nothing is impossible with God." (Luke 1:37)

Jesus got up, rebuked the wind and said to the waves, "Quiet! Be still!"
Mark 4:39

FAITH WORKS

Of what value is a faith you do not put into action? If it is mostly in your head, will it ever make it into practice? Living a life for Christ is only as good as it is tried and tested. "For no other foundation can anyone lay than that which is laid, which is Jesus Christ." (I Corinthians 3:11)

When troubles arise, what is your response? Can you stand with Me in spite of how you feel or the way things appear? As a believer, you are to "walk by faith, not by sight." (II Cor 5:7)

You always have the power of the Holy Spirit within you and My living word to support you, even if, at times, you believe you have nothing else.

Intellectual knowledge of Me has its place, but can easily be forgotten, debated, or denied, left to your own devices.

Stand in the truth of who you are: a child of God (Romans 8:16-17), free (John 8:36), prosperous (3 John 2), directed continually by God (Isaiah 58:11). Do not let this world shape you (Romans 12:2), for if you are not transformed by Me, you will conform to the ways of a dying world. (I John 2:16)

Do not give way to the enemy's lies that you are on your own. For I am with you. It is all too important to stand on the solid truth of who you are in Christ and to walk in this light each moment.

The world so easily wears you down with sin, trials, temptations, loss of hope, aimlessness. None of these flourish in Kingdom living.

My love for you has forgiven and redeemed you, made a way of escape (I Cor 10:13), given you hope and direction. (Jeremiah 29:11)

I hear your heart when you call to Me. "Do not fear...for from the first day that you set your heart to understand, and to humble yourself before your God, your words were heard; and I have come because of your words." (Daniel 10:12)

Faith is completed by works.
James 2:22

VICTORIOUS VIEW OF LIFE

In whom or what will you ultimately believe? Fix your gaze on the throne of God, who is the one true source of meaning and joy in this life and the next. How long will you go on believing in the ways of this world? They so subtly slip into your everyday thinking so as to rule your reactions in an ungodly manner.

You are called to respond to life events according to My Word ("Praise be to the God and Father of our Lord Jesus Christ, who has blessed us in the heavenly realms with every spiritual blessing in Christ." Ephesians 1:3)

Failing this, you are headed straight toward a fall into sin, discouragement, hopelessness, fear, anxiety—in short, a defeated view of life. Yet, I have called you to be victorious overcomers. (Psalm 18:35)

Why are so many of My beloved living without joy in the midst of My presence?

Repent for not believing in My Word—for chasing after false Gods. If it is not Me and My truth you choose to believe, then what have you chosen? And yes, it is your choice. You are not ruled by your emotions. Choose life. (Deuteronomy 30:19)

Be free in Christ as I have called you.

You give me your shield of victory.
Psalm 18:35

My Standard of Living

Living in and for the Kingdom of God involves continued attention on a much broader focus of how you live your life.

Do not be consumed by the minutiae of your everyday routines for they will pull you into the grasp of provincial living. Here you will concentrate mainly on self and either your pleasures or your pain. Pretty soon this will define your life as you choose to know it. Then your own problems become the worst calamities and crowd out compassion for others. Or your comfortable routine becomes a fortress you defend to stay in an easy life, indifferent to a deeper call to others.

Where are you? Are you able to look beyond your present circumstances and hear the voice of God? Do you still seek it? Or have you conformed to the small world of your own creation, void of My will for you? Check you standards for living. Have you compromised so much that they no longer challenge you to righteous living? Are they much different than the world's? What once shocked you—is that now acceptable? Return to your first love. (Revelation 2:4-5)

What is your life if not a shining light that pierces the darkness? Christ is in you. (Colossians 1:27) Represent him well. (II Corinthians 5:20)

I have chosen you out of the world.
John 15:19

PILGRIMAGE TO ETERNITY

Your current circumstances do not define you nor should they tint your view of Me in your life.

Only your faith and trust in Me should open your eyes at any given time to who you belong to. (Romans 5:1-2) You are mine and were created for Me. (Isaiah 43:1)

You are on pilgrimage to an eternal Heaven and this life is leading you there. Who are you to say what your life should be? (Job 42:1-5)

I have promised you all the joy, peace, hope, strength—when you believe and follow Me. (Romans 15:13) These same gifts are unavailable in this world outside of My grace.

This is why you can find joy in trials (James 1:2) or be despondent and empty in your self-claimed accomplishments. (Luke 9:25)

"And he said to me, 'My grace is sufficient for you, for My strength is made perfect in weakness.'" (II Corinthians 12:9)

Blessed are those whose strength is in you,
who have set their hearts on the pilgrimage.
Psalm 84:5

I Know Your Future

My will is a call to faithfulness that will lead you directly to My heart.

I am asking you to step out beyond the usual and the known, which, though comfortable, are not the pathways to My higher call for your life. (Proverbs 3:5-6) Though it may feel frightening to you as you step into the unknown, it is the best path to your ultimate joy and victory.

I give you My will as a command not to control, but because free will, left to its own devices, will always tend toward self without My clear guidance. I know your future. I know how to get you to the other side of your journey. "The Lord your God has blessed you in all the work of your hands. He has watched over your journey through this vast desert …The Lord your God has been with you, and you have not lacked anything." (Deuteronomy 2:7)

Stay close to My heart and you know My hand will follow. Stray from Me and, also, you will find My hand will follow, but to correct and direct. My will is intended to clarify and guide, not to hurt or encumber. Take it as such. I know what I'm about. Die to self, lose yourself in Me, and you will find the way to Me. Look for the cross and find the resurrection.

Put on the new self, created to be like God
Ephesians 4:24

The Anthem

"For My strength is made perfect in weakness." (II Corinthians 12:9)

Why then do you fight the weakness?

Like someone being saved from drowning who fights their rescuer, let go and allow yourself to be freed.

Don't confuse your talents and abilities as opportunities to take over My will for any situation. You are My vessel to be worked in and through. "You turn things upside down, as if the potter were thought to be like the clay! Shall what is formed say to him who formed it, "He did not make me"? Can the pot say of the potter, "He knows nothing"? (Isaiah 29:16)

Do not let pride or desire to control become your downfall. (Proverbs 16:18) There is no freedom in control.

Your trial times are typically My times to soar with you.

"He must become greater; I must become less" should be your anthem. (John 3:30)

Adversity will always be at your doorstep, causing the ground beneath you to feel unsettled. This will test your foundation and let you see where you stand in your relationship to Me. (Luke 6:48)

I am the God of light and darkness, for both are alike to Me. (Psalm 139:12)

My perfect love is meant to hold you and keep you from fear (I John 4:18) and it is always present in the strongest dimension regardless of how dour things may look.

Trusting in your own strength will give you reason to fear; surrendering your weakness to Me will provide you My strength, wisdom, and reveal to you the power of the living God in a much deeper way.

> *The Lord is My shepherd; I shall not lack.*
> *Psalm 23:1*

INTIMATELY AND INFINITELY PRESENT

"I do not pray for these alone, but also for those who will believe in Me through their word; that they all may be one, as You, Father, are in Me, and I in You; that they also may be one in Us, that the world may believe that You sent Me. And the glory which You gave Me I have given them, that they may be one just as We are one: I in them, and You in Me; that they may be made perfect in one, and that the world may know that You have sent Me, and have loved them as You have loved Me." (John 17:20-23)

Your hopes and dreams, trials and troubles are also My own.

I am intimately and infinitely present to you.

As deep as you sense your thoughts and feelings run, mine run deeper. Much deeper.

Yours glaze the surface, mine are like the depths of the ocean and carry with them My divine vision and power. As you pray and seek Me, I reveal glimpses of My eternal depths, whatever you need to take you through.

Just know that your prayers take you into My heart. I have already considered your situation to an infinite extent and felt what you feel beyond what you could ever know.

My love and My wisdom are intertwined when responding to your heart's cry.

Nothing happens by chance or without My infinite consideration.

Your attempts to take control by exercising your will exclude this, My loving intervention.

You could spend your entire earthly life pondering just one of your problems and still not give it the same consideration I do when you cry out to My tender heart.

I have known about all your concerns for millenniums and see your life fully unfolded before Me. Trust that My loving answer to you will be more than enough.

*Deep calls to deep
in the roar of your waterfalls;
Psalm 42:7*

Unleash My Mercy

"Mercy triumphs over judgment." (James 2:13) Does it in your life? How does mercy manifest in you? My life on earth was a living testimony to grace and mercy. I attempted to set the course for My people, but will they follow? ("If someone strikes you on the right cheek, turn to him the other also." Matthew 5:39)

How many opportunities for mercy were you faced with in just the last few days? How did you respond? Are you praying for your enemies? "You have heard that it was said, 'Love your neighbor and hate your enemy.'" But I tell you: Love your enemies and pray for those who persecute you, that you may be sons of your Father in Heaven. He causes his sun to rise on the evil and the good, and sends rain on the righteous and the unrighteous." (Matthew 5:43-45)

Do you forgive without hesitation, as I do for you? "Bear with each other and forgive whatever grievances you may have against one another. Forgive as the Lord forgave you." (Colossians 3:13)

Have you sought out the "undesirable" people who cross your path? What's holding you back?

You cannot be stingy with grace or it's not grace at all.

Forgiveness and mercy are not options for Kingdom living. They are calls.

They free you and unleash My flow of the same in your life. "And when you stand praying, if you hold anything against anyone, forgive him, so that your Father in Heaven may forgive you your sins." (Mark 11:25)

To crown Me Lord, live out My call. There is no better way to spread My message of love and truth.

You've been given the Holy Spirit to do so, not under your own power, but by My grace you can and will prevail.

> *If you love those who love you, what reward will you get?*
> *Matthew 5:44-46*

A Force For the Kingdom

"Teach me your way, O Lord, and I will walk in your truth; give me an undivided heart, that I may fear your name." Psalm 86:11

What good is the truth if you do not or choose not to embrace and activate it in your life? It is like having a banquet in the desert which you only look at and never taste. My Word is alive and powerful, invoking the presence of Jesus Christ into your life for whatever the occasion. (Luke 8:11-15)

Do not let your faith in Me become vain philosophy (Colossians 2:8), enticing to the intellect, but empty in its impact. Fear, anxiety, lack of peace are indicative of your being lukewarm on who I am. I can either make a difference in your life or I can't. Which will it be? My grace is still greater than your lack of belief. (II Corinthians 12:9)

I am God regardless of how anyone perceives Me. Your freedom and power come in standing on the truth of who I am: that My love for you is very real, that I am God alone, who works in your life moment by moment.

Do not let your trust in Me be so fragile that your faith ceases to be something that makes a difference in this world.

My Holy Spirit resides in you and I have plans for you to be a force for the Kingdom of God.

How you perceive that should be irrelevant if you have truly surrendered your heart and soul to My ways. Your fear and trepidation slowly eat away at your will. And, eventually, you give the enemy victory and paralyze My will, for I will not violate the gift of your will. But, should you choose your own path, you will inevitably face needless suffering. What you thought was protecting you will be leading you toward greater harm.

Learn from the parable of the lost son (Luke 15:11-31)—your ways are not My ways for very good reason.

My ways are guided by My love and omniscience. This has been My plan for you from the beginning of time.

This is truth. Follow it. Stand on it. Believe it.

For my thoughts are not your thoughts,
neither are your ways my ways.
Isaiah 55:8

EXCEEDING ABUNDANCE

Every good thing you have or ever had is a gift from your heavenly Father. (James 1:17)

My gracious supply is never earned nor can it be manipulated by your actions. Only faith, trust, and obedience move Me.

I am God of exceeding abundance (Ephesians 3:20) and endless provision. Could I ever disappoint you with My perfect gifts?

My love for you is perfect and entails My omniscient wisdom.

What I send is exactly what you need and more. Your degree of acceptance is up to you.

Will you embrace what I give in thanksgiving? Or complain that it isn't what you thought it would be? Or claim it as your due? Does your fear, impatience, or disappointment diminish your faith, which decreases your trust and leads you to seek your own disobedient "solution"? This speaks to your flesh and desire for worldly comfort. "But you are a chosen generation, a royal priesthood, a holy nation, his own special people, that you may proclaim the praises of him who called you out of darkness into his marvelous light." (I Peter 2:9)

What part does comfort of the flesh have to do with following Me? Who in the scriptures led a comfortable life who followed, trusted, and obeyed My call?

I am preparing you for My ultimate gift: eternal life with the Father, Son, and Holy Spirit. Be purified. (Matthew 5:8)

Keep your eyes fixed on the heavenly vision. (Acts 26:19) Take hold of the joy I am setting before you, joy that will last into eternity. (Hebrews 12:2)

Do you have any valid reason not to be joyful in light of your standing with Me?

Consider your difficulties the price to pay for Kingdom living. I am with you every step of the way—stay in step with Me and realize the joy I have always wanted you to live.

Mercy, peace and love be yours in abundance.
Jude 1:2

STAY VIGILANT

Never take My presence for granted and think that today is "just another day."

Your earthly, mindful thinking assumes you know what is in store for you. How will you know how to respond to My plan or an enemy attack if you have not fully put on you daily armor (Ephesians 6)?

Woe to you if you are caught off guard and miss an open door. My renewing of you is a daily, hourly event. Time is never wasted when you have given your life fully to Me. There are no days off in the Kingdom. "Let him who thinks he stands take heed, lest he fall." (I Corinthians 10:12)

The devil will lull you into false security with routine and habits of the flesh. Stay vigilant.

Be self-controlled and alert.
I Peter 5:8

GROW

How does a mature love show itself to this world?

It begins with mercy and seeks the good of others regardless of rewards or personal results. It is reflected by the countenance of the lover who lives peacefully amidst his enemies equally as among his friends.

True love lives to honor the living Lord and involves sacrifice and dying to your contrary ways. It is a steady flow, not based on your disposition, but on who I am. This love is not so much seen in the deeds you record, but in the emerging of the Holy Spirit within.

It is carried out in the hundreds of choices you make for righteousness each day when, clearly, other forces were telling you otherwise.

Mature love's end is not the pleasing of self or others; it is more the living manifestation and embodiment of Christ dwelling among us (John 1:14) "on earth as it is in Heaven." (Matthew 6:10)

Grow into your call for the divine, living love our Savior died for to change the world for him.

> *As they go on their way they are choked*
> *by life's worries, riches and pleasures,*
> *and they do not find fruition.*
> *Luke 8:14*

A Magnificent Life

Let your focus be on our relationship, for it is the paramount element of your existence. It will last into eternity. It grows with your surrender to My will. How easily you lose focus and treat the passing things of this world—which were mine to give you in the first place—with a greater importance. When our relationship is primary, you do not look to please others or place your trust in man. As you defer to My truth, the fruits of righteousness (Galatians 5:22) grow abundantly enough to consume and share.

Your earthly ties ultimately come down to you and what pleasure or pain they bring. This breeds selfishness and a utilitarian approach. With us, I don't need anything from you. I choose to want you and to love you. I will not placate you with what makes you feel good out of fear you'll reject Me. True love is willing to pay a price regardless of how things appear or feel. This life is passing. My love is meant to draw you closer to Me and I seek vessels who long to know Me without regard to the cost.

"Seek and you shall find..." (Luke 11:9) But don't look for Me on the beaten path. I will take you where you've never been before, leading you to a joy no one or no thing can corrupt. But, it may cause you pain and discomfort, however, "I am with you always." (Matthew 28:20)

Would you prefer earthly comfort without Me? Or the challenges that come with living for Me alone? "But if serving the Lord seems undesirable to you, then choose for yourselves this day whom you will serve..." (Joshua 24:15)

I want all of you and will not settle for a half commitment, which is none at all.

My mercy and grace are intended for your many shortcomings, but I'm looking for your heart. (Matthew 6:33)

Know that a life lived through Me is worth your existence.

Anything less will fall short of what I have planned for you. Come, know the magnificence of a life lived in and through Me.

The fruit of the Spirit is:
love, joy, peace,
patience, kindness, goodness,
faithfulness, gentleness and self-control.
Galatians 5:22

A Living Image

"For whom he foreknew, he also predestined, to be conformed to the image of his Son, that he might be the firstborn among many brethren." Romans 8:29. With whom or what do you attach your identity? Are you walking today as a child of God? You are "adopted as sons and daughters by Jesus Christ to himself, according to the good pleasure of his will." (Ephesians 1:5)

It was My choice that you would live this way. Before any of your time-limited earthly concerns became somehow paramount in your life, you belonged to Me. That has not changed. You are first and eternally My child, "For you were bought at a great price." (I Corinthians 6:20)

I want you to walk in My light, giving Me your first fruits of living—your time, your attention, your labors, your relationships—all of it is mine. If there is anything you covet, knowingly or unknowingly in your heart, anything that has consumed you, know that it is not from Me. I have called you to walk with Me and to let Me be in you. From this spiritual life, everything else will have its proper perspective.

I am not dismissing the relative importance of what occurs in your life, only that you see and receive everything through Me.

I can make your trials lighter when you seek Me first. (Matthew 11:28-30). I will increase the beauty of the things you value and keep them right in your mind and heart. You will have vision as you seek My direction. (Matthew 6:33) You will find purpose in your labors, hope in your trials, wisdom amidst your confusion.

Most of all, when you live as My child, you will know joy and fulfillment that is possible beyond earthly measure.

You are a living image of Jesus, one who works, struggles, loves, makes decisions, affects lives, grows older, prays, and so on. Not one who works, struggles, grows, et al only to consult with Me from time to time for "advice" on what you have already determined. Know who you are and live accordingly. It is a command, but is meant to direct you towards the divine life I have designed for you.

Do not miss it. Eternity begins now. Be an overcomer. Live joyfully in freedom from the world's ways. Nothing will ever be more important than our relationship, for I want you to know My all-encompassing love for you and for others that cannot be surpassed by any earthly endeavor.

He who believes in Me, as the scripture has said, out of his heart will flow rivers of living water.
John 7:38

PERFECTING MY BRIDE

Do you see your life as a call from Me and to Me?

Perhaps your current circumstances as submitted to Me are exactly where I want you. You say, "But how can sickness, oppression, pain, despair, aimlessness, boredom, etc., have anything to do with your holy will for my life?" Remember, this life is not about you.

At some point, didn't you tell Me, "My life is yours, Lord?" What did you mean by that? What did you think I meant by that? A life surrendered to Me is a life that builds My Kingdom according to My plan and timing. You mostly see this as acts of service to Me, but that is not the only way. My timing has much to do with it, too.

I am perfecting My bride.

How is it you want to serve Me, to love Me? Your way, so you can feel a sense of purpose for Me? Or will you take the way of the desert?

I am preparing you for eternity and My vision goes well beyond your time limited earthly existence. I love you too much to let you answer My call and not be in sync with My voice.

Along the way, I am perfecting you, amidst your pain, your boredom, your humbling situation.

What if you knew the situation I have brought you to were serving Me? Would you still want to change it? Could Daniel or Joseph have served Me in other ways? If I wanted them to. Did I exalt them? Were they in any position to exalt themselves for My glory? Only with My intervention—just as I would have it. Submission.

Think again what might it mean to Me. Ask the Holy Spirit if your life is submitted according to My will. Are you convicted by Me to move otherwise? If not, then stand ("…and having done all, to stand." Ephesians 6:13)

Standing may be difficult for you. Some would rather run 24-7 "for Me", than simply stay still "and know that I am God." (Psalm 46:10)

In your standing, look for Me—in the beauty of My creation, in the fellowship of loved ones, in praising and worshipping Me, in what grace I have given to help you overcome.

Whatever strength I've given you, walk in it today. Know that My call enfolds My tremendous love for you, even in the midst of your trial.

*I saw the Holy City, the new Jerusalem,
coming down out of Heaven from God,
prepared as a bride
beautifully dressed for her husband.
Revelation 21:2*

IMMENSE JOY

You have no idea to the degree I'm connected to you. If you did, you'd be hilariously joyful and peaceful.

Don't you know I'm connected to you in a way that guides your every step? I am there; I am here. I am with you and in you, no more so than in others, but I see you, and speak to you and through you. Find as you yield your way that life is less trouble, easier, as I'm leading the way toward greener pastures.

Your current circumstance bears little, if any, resemblance to where you're headed. I have great plans, a future and a hope.

You must face the wind for now. Bear up. Be bold and strong in My love, for I have not forgotten nor forsaken. Never have, never will. Trust more. Look to Me in doubts and fears. Always look this way—it is My light that shows the way, the path to abundant life. But the price is your life as you know it.

Are you ready and willing to surrender the average to Me for more of My life for you? I am God. Remember that. What can man do against My plans in a surrendered vessel, ready and willing to serve My Kingdom?

You will not always go away in despair and hopelessness. This is not the life I've chosen for My beloved.

There is immense joy behind this wall of the natural. If only you knew and could trust when I tell you what's there.

I am in control—is that not enough to rejoice in? God, the one who made it all, who makes it all happen with perfect rhyme and reason. Do you believe chaos has a place in the plans for My people? Nothing is haphazard, nothing without a reason and a purpose.

I am ever working My ways in and through you. You are vital to My call in this universe.

Let Me take it up for you. Let us run together and flee the ways of the past. Await, victory comes in the morning of My light. Live on!

> *No eye has seen, no ear has heard, no mind has conceived what God has prepared for those who love him.*
> *I Corinthians 2:9*

COMPLETE LOVE

Receive My love for you. Let it soak into you, and be absorbed in who I am. My light of love shines like no earthly love and is unlike what most deem love. It is not so much to be understood as it is to be experienced.

My love is not based on worth for all your worth is in Me, so it is a complete love, one that originates in the love of the Father, Son, and Spirit. It is this bond of powerful love that you are caught up in.

My power is in My love, a source so great nothing or no one can withstand it. Once touched, you can never go backwards for My love is pure, it draws, it heals, and cleanses. It is what all need to find their way in this broken world. To reject it is to be disembodied and wander, lost in an empty void.

I have pledged covenant love from My heart, where the truth of who I am to you comes forth.

Receive it—all of it.

> *Whoever lives in love lives in God, and God in him.*
> *I John 4:16*

SECTION TWO: INTERVIEW

This transcription is from the audio available at:
http://abundance.davenevins.com

—

Dave: O.K., are we ready?

Jim: Fire away, Dave. Here we are.

Dave: O.K., so welcome everybody. We are here. And we decided we're going to go partially anonymous with this, but that's not because of anything other than trying to reduce the social media.

Jim: *Amen.*

Dave: [laughter]

Jim: To God be the glory.

Dave: Amen.

All right, let's jump in. How did you start getting these messages?

Jim: The advantage for me is that I really didn't know what prophecy was—or basically really didn't even know what who God was, for that matter. [laughter]

I didn't know about any of this.

But, as I got to know the Lord—and just in praying with him, really tuning into him—you hear that prayer is a two-way street. So I would try to journal some stuff, and I eventually found that some of the things I journaled were—I don't know—they seemed a little different, like a message, like "Hmm, let's just kind of run with this a little bit."

I wrote down some things and some of them started coming quickly, and almost in the first person. I didn't really think anything of it. I just kind of wrote them down, recorded them, put them in my book. And I think shared some of them with you. So thanks to your encouragement Dave, I just said, "Oh, O.K., let's just see where this goes."

So in prayer time and just asking the Lord "Do you have anything to say? You know I've had my say plenty of times."

Then just kind of waiting.

And sometimes it just starts with a thought, or word, and I write it down in a sentence and then it just seems to come almost like a teleprompter. And then after you have got it all down, you kind of look back and say: "Hmm. That's interesting."

Then other people started to read them and said "Oh wow. I can relate to that." So it wasn't so much of like "this is my personal business out there". It was more like "maybe this is the Holy Spirit speaking universally". God has a way of saying things to us individually and corporately.

I think my confusion was that I was confusing that with the intimacy of God and that he is intensely personal to us in the way that is rarely seen in the world today.

Dave: So go back to the beginning before you started receiving these messages. Did you have a belief in God already? Good family?

Jim: Oh yeah. Great relationship with parents and siblings. Everyone got along pretty well. I always knew that Mom and Dad loved me. They were faithful churchgoers. They knew that Sunday meant it was time to go to church. But beyond that not much else in terms of "relationship." I never really heard that word as it related to God.

Dave: Going to church for you was a little more like paying taxes?

Jim: [laughter]

It's what you did; what you had to do as a kid, and I did not get a whole lot out of it. Although at some level—maybe it was the Holy Spirit speaking way back then—there was something more. I always sensed there was something else.

But spiritually there was nothing that would encourage me beyond Sunday church. It was all just stories and philosophy and blah, blah, blah—just nothing that really spoke to my spirit as I look back on it—to my core—that I guess was always there, but was left unfed.

And that lasted all through college and just beyond that. And then when I moved away from home, again I continued to feel a need for something else. It was just, not necessarily a need for the Lord, but just a need to stay connected; but not uber-spiritual.

As I was getting older, and kind of that sense of isolation you feel—just a sense of "How do I belong? Is there something bigger than me? I don't know what that is."

Then when I got out of college I moved away, far away. Being that far away with not a lot of natural worldly resources to lean on, I found myself trying to figure out "What am I doing here? Why am I here? What's my next direction?" I knew that somehow maybe praying would help. I think God was guiding me, but again in ways that I just really couldn't understand or know about.

Dave: Part of it then was that you just didn't know there was more.

Jim: Absolutely. Yes.

So then one time I met a friend. Clearly I could tell that she had a relationship—or something going on with God. Basically, I began to realize that there is something more. She would encourage me to come to her church. So I finally acquiesced and said "Y'know, I'll give it a shot." So I went, apprehensively, but as soon as I entered I knew something was going on in there.

There were people who were clearly experiencing the joy of the Lord. They were up on their feet, dancing, and singing and praising God.

Dave: You felt like they really were experiencing God. It wasn't just a circus.

Jim: Right. Folks were completely focused on the praise and worship. There didn't seem to be people distracted. The service was a bit longer than what I was used to, but it didn't feel that way. And the preaching was on the money; it was on the point; it was relevant.

Afterwards meeting the people it just seemed they were genuinely pleasant and sincere and interested in welcoming me to this church and asking about my journey with the Lord.

So that was just a very different experience for me. Again it wasn't just like "Hey, let's welcome the new guy." As soon as I walked in the door I just sensed something.

I couldn't put a name on it, but it was pretty cool.

As I look back, there were a lot of signs along the way. I continued to go to church and stayed in touch with my friend who said, "Y'know, what you need is a relationship with God." And I said "Well, I have a relationship with God. I think."

I'm like "How do I know? What does that mean, a relationship with God? What does that mean?"

And she tried to explain it: "We'll you hear from him. When you pray, you feel like he's moving in your heart. And all these other things. And she finally just said "Y'know, you really need to give your life to the Lord."

Again: "What does that mean? Give my life to the Lord? Haven't I been doing that for the last two or three decades? Maybe not."

So I said "All right I will pray the prayer and whatever." I remember doing that, from my heart; just basically committing my life to Jesus. Saying, "O.K., Lord, I don't know exactly what I'm doing, but I'm going to give it a shot. Here goes."

And then just that sense again of the Lord and his realness, and his presence—just a lot stronger.

And as I was hanging out with my friend she said "Oh, I notice a difference in you." I said "Really?" So I think it just kind of grew from there and just took off. The seed was planted and it started to blossom and I think was now open to more from God.

Well, obviously she had friends who were like her, as they say, "on fire for God." That wasn't me—yet.

There were no airs about them. They were sincere, laid-back, Southern California. Y'know—an immediate click that there's something about when you meet with other Christians—there's a connection there that's almost immediately deep.

And I think that's the thing I was looking for and I think a lot of people want truly meaningful relationships. And a lot of times people come and they go; so I think you gear your relationships that they are not going be around very long. But with Christians it was different. It was almost at the core of your being you immediately connect with somebody about just how important that is.

So y'know they would talk about things in a casual kind of way: "I'm hearing words form the Lord" or "I'm hearing this from God" or "God told me this" or "Let's pray about that," or "Let's drive this demon out."

Dave: [laughter]

Jim: Again they either assumed or didn't care that I was a novice to all this.

But it was fascinating.

And then they would be wanting to pray over me a lot, and they would pray and would start to get words or visions or things for me, about me, about things that I was concerned about.

And the words started to speak to me. I think when the words came—they spoke to *me*.

A lot of times the words were stuff like, "Well, I'm not sure about this, but the Lord is saying…" and it spoke directly to me, as opposed to them just saying what they think. And that was what made me raise an eyebrow and say "Hmm. Interesting. Now how would you possibly know that about me? How could you know that that is something meaningful to me?" So it was almost inherent, the things that they were saying that we're just so deep.

I went to one of their churches and there was a prophet there. I thought, "This ought to be interesting." And she was praying over people and said "Come on up," like something you would picture in the New Testament when Jesus showed up. So this woman who—out of the blue, didn't know anything about me—at the time I was thinking about going to graduate school, and people were pooh-poohing that: "I don't know; it's too expensive, da-da-da." And when she was praying over me, getting these words, and then just as she was done, she said, "Oh, and another thing: You have been thinking about wanting to go to school. Well, the Lord says go for it!" [laughter] I was just like "Whoa." I mean this woman I'd never met her—didn't know anything—that was it. That kind of blew me away. That was just one example.

Dave: And there have been many, right?

Jim: Yeah. Oh yeah, there have been many. But that was probably one of the first.

I think that he definitely wants to speak to us about things that we need to know about. And that was a key component that led to my career path. So he wanted to make sure I was tuned in.

So with all these awesome things going on, all my friends getting these words and visions—y'know I wasn't quite there yet. I had just come to know God and I did feel my relationship with him was building.

My friends could kind of sense, "You need a little bit more here. So get up here! We're gonna pray for you right now and you can receive more of the Holy Spirit." And they laid hands on me, prayed, and were praying for the gift of tongues—which is another gift in itself.

Dave: After that prayer you started experiencing more?

Jim: Yeah. My prayer time felt like it was more of a two-way street now. I was definitely hearing from God in ways that I hadn't before. Scripture just came alive—like it was jumping out of the Bible at me. The truth that's in there that's just unpacked as you read it was just so much more profound.

Dave: So God was speaking to you with more clarity, but it wasn't as clear as it would become?

Jim: Correct. Yes. Definitely prayer life was getting much stronger. It wasn't until later that the words or visions started to come.

And I guess it was with the fellowship of other Christians who had received similar gifts or who we're much more aware of it than I, the encouragement and confirmation was, "Hey it sounds like maybe you have that gift of prophecy." Which initially when I heard that, I'm like, the kind of question of "who am I?" It's really hard to envision yourself as being that voice, or seeing these things, and truly believing that this is God.

Well, Dave, you were a big encourager to me.

It just would come in prayer time, or sometimes not even in prayer time. You would be riding your bike, or whatever, and something would come and it would be like just a quick sentence or a phrase, or what seemed like a thought.

I could get to the point where I would say, "Alright Lord, I'm open to whatever you want to tell me."

Dave: Well, don't overthink it. [sarcastically]

Jim: [laughter] Yeah. So I started to write. I would just write a little bit more, and a little bit more…

And it almost kind of took on a life of its own, in a way, as you wrote it.

Dave: So there was a transition between it feeling like you were generating it, and the Holy Spirit generating it in you.

Jim: Yes.

Dave: And for you journaling helped set the environment?

Jim: Right. Some people will get them and just speak them out and could speak for minutes. I felt that "I need to write this down, because I'm definitely getting some input here."

And I guess it was that sense of like "O.K., the Lord is trying to speak here." Which again, I think it's a matter of time. As your relationship grows with the Lord, I think God is ready to give us whatever gifts. He's got them in abundance there, clearly.

So I think as the relationship builds, it was a matter of kind of stepping out a little bit, personally, saying "O.K., maybe the Lord does want to speak to me this way. I mean he could speak in so many ways. Why wouldn't he want to speak?"

So I would just try to write down what I felt was being spoken to me. It wasn't like I was taken over. It was still my thoughts, but definitely *highly inspired thoughts,* shall we say, that as I was writing it down, clearly aware of what I was writing down, even to the point where if I had spelled something wrong I could be like "O.K., I can fix that." The conscious mind is definitely still there.

As I would go back and read, it was just interesting, because there were some points in there that seemed perhaps more profound or deeper than something I personally think I could have written, clearly speaking to me at another level. I think it makes things more clear.

You know, not only do I feel that God is behind this, these words couldn't be any clearer in a lot of ways.

They seem to have an ongoing relevance.

The underlying theme in just about all of them is God's love and caring for me—that he is with me now and he will be with me.

I can take that any time. I can take that into the future. I can realize that it was a part of my past; that he is speaking here and now from all eternity.

There's something pretty powerful about that to me.

Dave: Are you glad you have this gift?

Jim: [laughter] Yeah. I think you've even sent me a couple of them and I'm like, "Oh, who wrote that Dave?" And you said, "Well, you did." [laughter] But it's all Holy Spirit, just working in and through us, so I'm grateful for those words.

Well, I find that those words are consistent with God's Word. Certainly, like you said, it's not adding to anything. In a lot of ways—how can I say—they "act" like the Word.

I mean I've gotten words that have been words of correction to me. Lots of those! [laughter] But I don't feel condemned and God is saying something and it's always intertwined with supporting me and that he's with me and how much he loves me. You know there will be sometimes reminders of specific instances in the Bible.

Dave: So he takes the Bible and shows you how it applies to your life.

Jim: Yes. Well there's only so much I think you can do with the data that you receive from life itself. You take it; you think about it; you ask people about it. But when you start to take it to prayer, God longs to speak to us and give us direction. And his will for our life I think is much greater than what we want. You know we're always saying "What is your will God? Show me."

And I found that the words that he has given me give much more depth, especially nowadays where time is lacking, or we just want all our answers right away from our smart phone or a tablet or whatever.

Spending that time with God allows him to speak, taking things and bringing depth to them.

Once you know him you can't get enough.

--

Dave: In this part we'll talk more specifically about gifts.

Jim: God does gift each of us with certain gifts. It is not something to fear or be boastful about. The bigger picture is God just wanting to speak to our hearts. And however he chooses to do that, whomever he chooses to do it through, is really up to him. It's up to us to accept that and to receive it, and to share it with others.

You know there's plenty of people with the gift, and as you speak with others or experience that, you see some similarities in how people receive the gift or how they share it. [It's] a little bit of encouragement, which hopefully this talk does for those hearing it.

God can do anything, and he can speak through any of us. It's just the willingness to do that, and our surrender to whatever he wants.

Dave: What is your routine? I remember I used to see you in that rocking chair doing soaking, chill prayer.

Jim: Mmm.

I think you sit down in your prayer time and you spend some time with the Lord, a little prayer and praise, scripture reading. And then just try to keep your mind uncluttered, asking the Lord to speak. Maybe he gives you a scripture or something that you read and it almost kind of lightens up. I don't know how else to put it, but it kind of jumps out.

And then it's like "Oh, is that that what you want Lord? You want to tell me something about that?" And then it's like "O.K., we're rolling."

And then the Lord just starts to speak. And it's always helpful to have a pen and a paper or a tablet or whatever it is.

From there it just seems to flow out.

I think if it's happening to you, you'll know. It's more than just something that you're just thinking about. You usually don't come to the table with something like "I want to write about this." It is often a topic that's pertinent, relevant, typically to yourself.

I guess as I got used to it, that's when it became more first person. I would write "God is telling me this" and "He's telling me that." As I went on it just seemed to flow more naturally that this is the Holy Spirit speaking. Sometimes it would be intertwined with scriptures that I would know, or even ones that I didn't know that well, that would just kind of flow in there.

Very personal though—the Holy Spirit speaking from the heart to the heart.

It's really cool actually.

Dave: I noticed these developed into more eloquent, poetic, stylized writings.

Jim: I think as you open up a bit more, you're like "Hmm, I think really the Holy Spirit is trying to speak."

Part of it is getting over the idea that "why would he speak to me?" and "who am I?" So there is this false humility.

I think once you realize you're getting a download—sometimes you'll pray and you'll get like a phrase, a scripture—that's kind of it. But when the words come, it's kind of like, what is it—a stenographer? Like "O.K., let me get this down" and it then just starts to flow. Sometimes, you know, it's shorter, a paragraph, a page; but you read it back and it surprisingly makes sense.

Dave: So as far as how it sounds, it has the nature of your own thoughts, but it just doesn't sound like you originated it. It has that sense of surprise about it, where you are *spoken to*.

Jim: Yeah, there's definitely a difference there. Something comes in and it's certainly something you weren't even thinking about, and it comes in and—and the only way I can describe it is that its like a thought—well, I don't want to say implanted, but I don't know how else to say it—it's something that you know really didn't come from you.

And the Holy Spirit puts it in there, but then once it's in there, it just kind of starts to grow.

Dave: And you also have this other prophetic gift of seeing visions.

Jim: Oh the visions. I get visions mainly when I pray for people.

Dave: You get them quite a bit.

Jim: Oh, definitely.

Dave: These things just aren't produced by a couple of glasses of Guinness.

Jim: [laughter] Hardly.

Dave: For example, you can change the interpretation of what you received, but not the actual content.

Jim: Yes.

Dave: And sometimes to get the meaning of what he's trying to say, you might actually have to pursue God, by asking questions or waiting.

Jim: Right. You'll be praying and there's an image of something that pops in and you will say, "What was that, Lord?"

Dave: How do you know you're not being distracted by your imagination?

Jim: You know it's different than a distraction. Distraction I think is more something that is of your memory or something that you're more conscious of, versus the genesis of a vision seems to be the Lord's way of saying "Hey." It gets your attention. Then you kind of dig into it. You see that all the time in the Bible. You look at the dreams Daniel had.

Dave: And your wife actually gets a thing called prophetic dreams: where they are more vivid; they don't "jump cut"; you sense that they are from God; they come true. She gets a lot of different things, right?

Jim: Words of knowledge.

Dave: Yeah. Explain what a "word of knowledge" is please.

Jim: Basically it's the Lord implanting a knowledge about a situation that you would otherwise not possibly have means, or access, or understanding of. The Lord tells you something and you know that you know that you know. And the proof of the pudding is in the sharing of it. And it's usually spot on.

Dave: Yeah, and if you're new to this, one of the tricky parts can be—sometimes the visions are symbolic and sometimes they're literal—or both.

Jim: Yeah, sometimes you see things that are like "Well—what was that?"

Dave: I remember that vision you had of all those angels.

Jim: Oh yeah.

Dave: Tell us about that one.

Jim: As I recall, we were praying; it was just a lot of us in the room praying—and then a vision of a big area, thousands of angels all ordered, in mini-rows, and periodically one would peel off and take off. It just seemed to be in the midst of a spirit of praise and worship, almost like we were caught up with them in that.

Dave: We have a mutual friend and I asked her to pray for this book and she said she had a vision of angels. And they may have been the angels that you saw because they were saying "Hey—look at this. We're in a book."

Jim: [laughter] It's about time!

Dave: [laughter] Kinda fun, huh?

Jim: I believe that book would be Bible, Dave. They are in that book too.

Dave: Yeah. There's a lot of things in that book.

Jim: Y'know, another time we were praying and there were some demons in the room, checking us out, like, "What are you doing?" And believe me—that came out of nowhere. I mean that was like "Whoa."

Dave: Did you sense a darkness with that?

Jim: Yeah. Y'know, not like a pressing sense of danger, like *The Exorcist* or something, just a recognition of the existence of that realm. As if you witness something visually and you see it and you almost get the holograph of it—I remember that.

Dave: He shows us what's going on behind the curtain.

Jim: Yeah. And also too you just get the sense of God's power. It's not like a nightmare or dream where you are like, "Oh my God, the devil is going to kill me" or something like that. It is more like "Wow", just this glimpse of the awesomeness of God that's like "Whoa".

Dave: They were the ones that were afraid.

Jim: Yeah. Kind of huddled, almost like "We need to be careful."

Dave: Exactly. You must have had hundreds of visions in your life.

Jim: [laughter] I haven't counted them lately, Dave. Maybe.

Dave: I think it's fun when two people will get the same vision.

Jim: Mm-mm.

Dave: Or some other external confirmation.

I remember I was at your house for dinner and you and your wife offered me this boatload of strawberries—which I never eat. But I did. And then on the way home I was praying over the phone with another friend—not having any clue about my dessert or where I had been—and she gets a prophetic word and didn't have any idea what it meant. It was just one line where Jesus said to her: "Ask Dave, *What is it about you and strawberries?*"

Jim: [laughter] Yeah, well I think it speaks to the sense of humor that the Holy Spirit has. Y'know God is a lot of fun, when you think about it.

Dave: He's not just serious.

Jim: I think he just does stuff to say, "Yeah, I'm more in tune than you realize," because we certainly limit him by our brain.

Dave: And you introduced me to a bunch of friends of ours, some missionaries from Zambia.

Jim: Mm-mm.

Dave: And a lot of the words that you received came from those prayer sessions, which were often long and deep.

Jim: Yeah.

Dave: Although you don't have to have a long and deep session to get a prophetic word. It can happen even when you're not asking for it.

Jim: Sure.

Dave: But the deep worship helps a lot.

Jim: And they were pretty hard-chargers there. A two-hour prayer meeting was just warming up. You don't realize how quickly the time can go when you really get that deep in with what the Lord reveals.

There is a gift in the air when you spend that much time with the Lord on a consistent basis. You're going to see it, eventually.

Again not to say that that is the only way, but any time we commit to the Lord to spend time with him, he is going to reveal himself. It's his nature.

Dave: Now I remember my first impressions of our friends from Zambia. Normally you get the greeters. And all I remember was a bunch of repentant posteriors pointed toward the sky, and a lot of hunger for God.

Jim: [laughter] Yeah, there was no welcoming committee.

Dave: I preferred that.

Jim: Yeah.

Dave: Because I wanted to be in an environment where people were more hungry for God than they were for converting me.

Jim: Right. I don't even think they realized you were there until an hour in.

Dave: Until they left.

Jim: [laughter]

Dave: In case they should happen to hear this, is it time for you to fess up about that special bizarre tambourine that you hid because you got distracted?

Jim: [laughter]

Dave: Tell us about that tambourine for the record. They're going to find out in Heaven anyway.

Jim: [laughter] Oh.

Dave: You were getting these really cool prophetic words and one week they started to break out this very peculiar tambourine that was extremely distracting and you couldn't focus. Somehow it ended up under the sofa cushion and then magically reappeared months later. We couldn't handle the secret anymore.

Jim: Yeah, I did—but did not fess up at the time. So, true confession.

Not to say that tambourines can't be part of your praise and worship. I could have handled eggs or shakers.

Dave: Well, that tambourine in particular would call down a lot of angels. We know that. [sarcastically]

Jim: [laughter] Yeah, you know, I'm an INFP.

Dave: Speaking of the personality type INFP, would you say that your words are harder on you perhaps because you are laid back, whereas if somebody has more emotional damage, like a rescue puppy, then God might speak to them more gently?

Jim: Yeah, I think any word that I got always felt like it was for me first, but the fact that others resonate with them I think speaks more that we share a lot of concerns, anxieties, fears, doubts, victories, etc. But I was just surprised. I mean, they are so personal.

Prayer time with God is like a laser. A little bit of God is a lot. And he can do what he needs to do in the time that you give him.

Dave: Including intense rest.

Jim: Including intense rest, yeah.

But I must say that the words or visions for me at least—I could be hiking or biking or swimming, or whatever—it's really just openness. I guess if you're open, then God can speak to you anywhere, anytime.

Dave: I think the key is having the right heart and being for hungry for God. You have that hunger, and everybody that knows you really loves you.

Jim: Hope so.

Dave: So having the right heart is more important than seeking a gift.

Jim: Yeah. You know none of us are perfect. Clearly we all have our sins, some more glaring than others. That is probably the biggest thing used against you by the enemy, like "what are you talking about this for?"

Dave: Yeah, Jesus calls him the Accuser.

Jim: But a lot of times the very words are the things—the convicting words—are the things coming to me because of those shortcomings.

Dave: They are part of the way out.

Jim: Yeah. I think there was another confirming thing with the words themselves was that God never really spanks you on the bottom without giving you a hug at the same time.

Dave: [laughter]

Jim: There was never a thing that was like "Oh, I feel awful." I could not correct something, or quite say it in a way that I think the words should come out.

Dave: Do you feel like the words you got are more eloquent than you can write on your own?

Jim: Yeah, I'd say they'd be edited, occasionally a word here, or punctuation there, but they are surprisingly complete in how they come out. I've never gotten something that afterwards I was like "Huh?"

I've never been that "inspired" to write a word that wasn't from the Lord. You know what I mean? I'm too lazy I guess.

I find the two very different.

Dave: O.K., what about this? If a person has a father, let's say, who was very angry, they may hear the difficult parts of these words more loudly, and not hear the tender parts.

Jim: Absolutely.

Dave: So tell us about how you hear the tone of God's voice. Y'know, in the Bible we can get the words of King David's psalms, but not the music. Similarly, you heard not just the words, you heard the tone. How would you describe that?

Jim: It's just always very encouraging. Yeah. It's never condemning.

The sense I get from the Lord is that:

"The reason I am making this aware or telling you about it, is not to chastise or castigate you, or whatever. It is to let you know that this is in some way blocking what I want to do for you."

God mourns over our sin more than he shakes his finger at us. The earthly sense that we often get is that we are bad and because of this something bad is going to happen. But the words are just very encouraging and uplifting.

It's like "O.K. you did this, this is a problem, but I love you and My Word says this…"

If we think we are bad or that we should be punished, I think it misses the point of who God really is. You know the whole reason Jesus died is to keep us out of condemnation so that we can live in his love.

The sense I was got was that "you know I love you matter what. And I'm there. There's so much more to Me and to My kingdom. Don't get caught up or lost in what you see and what you are currently experiencing in this temporal realm. You do exist in that but you also are part of the eternal realm. If only you could see the other side and what that's like, you'd be astonished."

John alludes to that in the gospel.

It's easy to lose sight of that in our daily issues, concerns, and stressors. And it is helpful to have that reminder that God is ever present.

And not just present but he just loves us so much. On our best and our worst day, whatever. He is consistent.

It's just very encouraging.

And the cool thing—I mean, you've been so kind Dave to chronicle all these words—and I've read back on them and they maintain that sense, that power.

You're like "Wow. Still true?"

--

Dave: In this last part we'll talk about specific prayers anyone can access to increase the ability to hear. And at the end, and most importantly, rather than just talk about God, we'll wrap up by talking with God.

One of the practical things we can do is this prayer Christ used placing hands on the person. And during that it can be offered as something the Bible calls the Baptism in the Holy Spirit. How would you encourage somebody else with this? What happened to you?

Jim: Well, I was still new in all the things of the charismatic, Holy Spirit nature. So my ignorance was bliss. I was hanging out with contemporaries who had known the Lord for years. But they were hard-chargers. They were getting visions, and words and healings and mission work, all that stuff. So they said "Oh, so you don't have the gift of the Holy Spirit?" Almost indignant. "Hey, get over here! We're going to pray for you." [laughter] So they just put me in the middle of the room there and just laid hands.

Dave: They basically sat you down, prayed with you and then?

Jim: And then went back to what they were doing.

Dave: And you had this life changing experience!

[laughter]

Jim: Yeah. I had the glow of the Holy Spirit.

Dave: One guy acted as if he had just delivered a baby, and finished smoking a cigarette.

Jim: Yeah. I think it was within the same cigarette. I hought, "Wow." He puts it down, prays, I get filled. He goes right back to his cigarette, almost like he didn't miss a beat in the conversation. [laughter] I'm like "Wow—what just happened to me?" "Hey, pretty cool, yeah?" "Yeah." "All right, let's go get some food." [laughter]

Dave: What essentially happens in this prayer, the Baptism of the Holy Spirit? They put hands on you. You basically ask God for more of his presence and gifts.

Jim: God gets more of us, so they say in the Baptism of the Holy Spirit. You receive him in a "charismatic" sort of way, or whatever you wanna call it. Sometimes people get caught up in that. It is more about why wouldn't you want more? But you definitely—I definitely—noticed a difference when that happened.

It just makes you more aware.

It tunes you in to stuff, I think—different things in the supernatural that you couldn't possibly imagine or believe—some of the things you hear or see, and the ability to pray in tongues.

Dave: Yeah, tell us about that. The Bible says it's actually God praying for you.

Jim: So often we pray, you know at a certain point, words seem to almost get in the way. So the praying in tongues was really kind of cool, because you can do that for a long time, as you know.

Dave: It's much easier for this thing called "praise", which is a celebration or a party for God, with God.

Jim: It is. It is.

Dave: Now, did you get the gift of tongues at the time they prayed for you for the Baptism in the Spirit?

Jim: Yeah, I did, which I know isn't always the case for everybody, but for me it was.

Dave: Do you have any practical advice for receiving the gift of tongues? Obviously, you have to start praising God out loud and trust, and then at some point it uncorks, like opening a bottle of wine.

Jim: People praying with you I think helps a lot, certainly, because people already have the gift. I think they kind of think back about when it happened to them. Not to say that you couldn't receive it in and of yourself in your prayer time, but would you know what it is, what it looks like? I think a practical part is: "How will I know? What does it look like? Sound like, etc.?" I think that's a practical step to it, certainly.

And, you know, not to be discouraged, whether it's "I do not have enough faith" or "I'm this…"

Dave: And then regarding visions you had received a few of them, but then our friend Keith and I prayed with you doing the laying on of hands prayer, specifically asking God to release more of them. Then that's when they really started to increase.

Jim: Mm-mm. If you don't have a fellowship of believers around you, especially people who've been around, who know what that is, because otherwise it can be a little scary, it can be a little odd.

Dave: Yeah, anytime you go through a major change.

Jim: Mm-mm

Dave: If we don't have the protection and provision of God as a good Father, we can very easily *become our own Father*, instead of letting him do that.

Jim: When that doesn't happen the result can go many ways. I think one of which is that you take your problem and then you try to either justify it or normalize it. And we all have the same problems. Lacking that guidance, we will just say "Well, I think this is the way I am."

Dave: But if we know we have a Father that's committed to us, then we can re-commit back.

Jim: Yeah. That commitment is the thing that really opens the door to God, because he's gracious and he honors our free will.

Our response to that is often akin to how much hurt we still hold onto or how much we choose willingly or unwillingly to hold on to what ever that issue is.

Dave: And when we let go, God shows us gifts we don't even know we have, like the gifts you've been given.

Jim: Well and the sad thing is that God has something for everybody, and it can lay dormant for years, or for a lifetime, sadly.

And without that love of the Father to guide us along and encourage us—it's that parallel to the earthly father. If your earthly father didn't know how to encourage you or build you up, then what did you do, did you not perform, or underperform, or overperform?

But I think the whole idea of wanting to become a part of something bigger than ourselves—unless you are completely narcissistic—you realize that it is good to be part of a whole. The Christian faith is very much so that way. It can support you; it can correct you; it can encourage you.

Certainly when you give him your life, get ready, because even in the ordinariness of everyday life there's a certain flair to it, when you know the Holy Spirit.

There's an appreciation for the simple. There's a willingness to do things that you couldn't have thought you would've done, everything from getting married, to getting this job, or living in this area, or "How can I do this on this much money?", or you name it. "How can I do this with my shortcoming—I'm too dumb, too ugly, too shy."

Dave: You say shy? Don't you mean more coy, or diffident, demure, prim?

Jim: [laughter] Huh?

Dave: I know you love colorful words.

Jim: Ahh. Obsequious.

Dave: But what could be better than God? It's just that we have the wrong idea. For some reason we can think he's a jerk. So we need a serious detox for that. The truth is nobody feels our joys and sorrow and dreams more than he does.

Jim: Amen. I think he just seems so abstract to many people, but the manifestation of it becomes so evident, it is really hard to think any other way. You see the fruit of it in your life, and in other people's lives and you're like "Wow".

I just can't imagine my life without the Holy Spirit.

Otherwise what is the purpose? A life can become sometimes difficult, but it can also be very ordinary. Sometimes the ordinariness leaves you thinking, "What else? Now what? Am I doing what I am supposed to be doing?"

You know a lot of times God is like "You're right on. Keep doing what you're doing, and *be ready.*" You never know what God's got for you.

Dave: I think a lot of times we don't realize that we may be *already* pleasing God and he has to tell us.

Jim: True. That is why they have these things called prophetic words.

Dave: It's hard to believe sometimes that God likes you or is proud of you.

Jim: Where else do you get that in life really? Even good parents and spouses and children, whatever, aren't always that forthcoming with that, and God is that way every day, which I think allows you to take that into your life.

And that's pretty amazing.

Dave: Would you call that "surrendering to abundance"?

Jim: Surrendering to abundance, Dave. That's it. John 10:10.

—

Dave: We're going to finish with a prayer, if that's O.K.

Jim: Sure.

Dave: Alright here we go. So God, we thank you. We trust you, God. You're the best.

Jim: Lord, we just pray that you release the power of your love in our hearts. However we have experienced you in our lives, we ask you now for that touch, to take us to where it is you want us to be.

Dave: Yeah, Lord we let the Spirit inside us guide us.

And we give to you our weaknesses, and addictions, and sins, and we ask you, "What do you give us, instead of these?"

Jim: Whatever is inhibiting us from our past, from our atmosphere, from our surroundings, we just pray for release from that and just to surrender to you. Anything holding us back: we just let go of that.

We welcome you, Lord. We thank you that you are our love. We want to know what you have for us. So come. Fill us up. Fill our hearts. Surprise us, Lord. Just give us your joy, your peace, your hope, your strength, and your wisdom. Come Lord. We just welcome you right now.

We thank you that you have done the work. You have accomplished it already. You have forgiven us, and now Lord we ask you to complete that forgiveness in us.

It's not how we see ourselves or how others see us. It is what you see us as.

Let us be set free, from anything else that is not from you.

Let us begin our eternity with you now. And begin to share in the love that you designed us for, that you created us for. We thank you for it.

Dave: Yeah God, we specifically, directly ask you, to reveal more of yourself to us. We want more of you.

Yeah, show us more of your glory.

[praying in tongues]

I feel something stirring right now.

What do you see?

Jim: Just this image of Jesus, kind of, with a big joyful look on his face—Jesus' joy.

He is laughing. He is kind of welcoming people in, kind of calling them up, welcoming, welcoming people. Anyone who says "Yes" in any way—he is just so delighted to hear that.

Like the Prodigal Son where God is coming running to us. He is just waiting. He is so eager for that "Yes." He will honor our will.

He's just so—just this sense of excitement and joy, love. He's just like, "I have so much and I just want to share it. And the more people that come, the more I can do that."

It's almost like it expands exponentially with every person that comes in the Kingdom and then it just flows over to everybody else.

So much joy. So much laughter. He just wants us to come.

Not to minimize the issues and sadness that exist in this world, but God is—he is beyond that.

And he is just—he is still joyful. He is still loving.

And he is, for lack of a better word, excited, and desirous of us.

And he is ready to start the banquet, so, he said he's done all the work, just come and enjoy. Enjoy him.

Well you know, you look at all the suffering in the world. Why is God so joyful?

Dave: Well, he can see over the hill. He knows the endgame.

Jim: Well, he does.

Hmm.

He's up on the hill and he's just welcoming people, and it's like he's trying to gather as many people together, like "Come on!" as if there was just something up above where he wanted people to be and see it.

Like, "Don't miss this. This is awesome." Like everybody who is here is having a great time and enjoying it, and loving it. It's just so genuinely great. You don't wanna miss it. Kind of "You don't wanna miss it" thing.

Dave: That was the strongest part of it?

Jim: Yeah. Just a lot of joy. Laughter.

Not just—joy sometimes feels amorphous—just this genuine, "Wow I'm so happy—here."

--

Dave: All right, great. Thank you, God.

So we'll just wrap up here and say, "In Christ's name we pray."

Jim: Amen.

Dave: Awesome. Thank you very much. All right. Thanks for doing this. Appreciate you and all you've done.

Jim: My pleasure, Dave. Thank you for sharing for the Kingdom.

Dave: O.K., we're going to sign off. Thank you for tuning in and listening.

Cheers.

[glasses clink]

Jim: Colonel.

Dave: Signing off.

Jim: Sayonara.

SECTION THREE:
RECEIVING AND GIVING MESSAGES

Lessons Learned—Dave Nevins

Here are some of my discoveries on gifts that help discern the voice of God's love.

There's a lot covered here, given mainly to help trigger further exploration, so it's fine to just casually browse around. Use what you want. These are just a bunch of things I wish someone had told me sooner.

We'll start with a broad overview and then go into more specific tips. Along the way I'll share some of my own experiences.

(These points are presented in a conversational Q&A format to help readability.)

3.0—HISTORICAL OVERVIEW

What is your background?

In brief: I was raised near Washington D.C. in a good-hearted, talented, entertaining Irish family. Though I've always been a believer, my major disappointment with God was that he was no longer interacting with the world today as in biblical times, except in obvious emergencies. It never occurred to me that this might not be true. I felt it was really too bad, because being able to hear God's guidance would be a master advantage in life.

A few simultaneous trials in my early twenties caused me to pursue the Lord more vigorously, but even those efforts didn't seem to have much effect on my circumstances. This was puzzling because I thought I was doing all the "right things."

At the time I would have definitely labeled myself as Christian, and perhaps I was, but the examples of friends who were much more unmistakably sold out for Christ inspired me to completely commit myself.

Immediately following that, I had a few breakthrough episodes of distinct contact with God, which were unexpected because I was asking primarily for relief from pain. Apparently God was after my heart first! I had known he would answer 911 calls; but the cell line was nicer.

Those incidents set me on a quest for more. What you are now reading is a result.

So I have a heart for those who assume their only option is resignation to unknown forces of suffering. It's a pleasant epiphany that Jesus actually loves to proclaim God's favor. [Luke 4:18]

Let's plunge in.

Where do we start?

Here's some context:

The messages included in this book represent examples of a clearer, more direct form of hearing God, referred to in Christianity as the gift of "prophecy." This is a legitimate, active, modern gift; but the term brings along a few misconceptions, as we'll see below.

The Bible talks about prophecy as one of many different supernatural abilities called "charisms" (from the Greek meaning "special gift"—as in someone with a charismatic personality).

Prophecy is just one of several gifts?

Yes, and even within the prophecy gift set, there are varieties of types. Sometimes what we get won't always be what we expect!

For instance, I am always impressed by friends who receive first-person word-for-word messages, such as the ones in this book, but it wasn't until later in life that I discovered I also have a prophetic gift buried in my unconscious emotions. Its type is not well-known, but is an empathic power to feel God's feelings for another, sometimes including bodily sensations.

It was an odd surprise since I'm not a touchy-feely person, as you might guess. In fact, being Irish, I had considered my prophetic ability to be less foresight and more hindsight. ;)

You don't hear a lot about emotional gifts.

Even though our culture doesn't publicly place high value on feelings, Jesus obviously showcased the emotional God: Think of the Passion of the Christ, the Resurrection, Pentecost, etc. These are loaded with total impact. We can't have God's fullest love without it.

In fact, we may even sometimes think God is unsympathetic, when in reality no one's feelings are richer and deeper.

This is important to know. because it's a shortcut to his heart, rather than looking for a technique.

Experiencing God's emotions is consequential. Jesus was "moved" into more power [Matt 14:14]. That's one massive reason to connect with God in that way.

"My heart moves My hand."

Before we go on, how are you qualified on these topics?

I'm qualified only in the sense everyone is: by relaying personal experience, like many do all over the world.

The great thing here is that anyone can approach God to learn to recognize whatever gifts are lying inside. That's one thing I love about it. It's so easy to encourage. God backs it up. It's definitely not about one person being better than another.

However, one ability I've experienced consistently over the years is that when I pray for others, they will often hear God much more clearly than before. So I can share that. For instance, when I place my hands on others in prayer it's very common for them to see visions of angels—yet ironically, I've never seen one.

Does anyone think you are arrogant?

Actually, I can understand the concern! When a person is talking about God in a passionate way, it's hard to be completely confident, yet also thoroughly humble; to be sure about what is true, yet always pliable to admit where you might be wrong. But of course, that's the case regardless of what you care about. So there's no qualification for being convinced about who you love.

When it comes to Christianity I think the solution is to reroute as much as I can to Christ, so that it's not about me, but about him. That's the goal anyway. The more we can do that, the better.

I am perfectly happy to say "do whatever he tells you," [John 2:5] because then the reader can access this without feeling pressure.

Like kids, each one of us reflects a unique, God-inspired glory that says, "Hey, check it out."

What are some other gifts?

If you have made it this far in the book, I'll assume you probably won't flinch from these other related powers described in the Bible.

These might initially seem like curious phenomena—yet I vouch for them based on my own non-trivial, first hand participation. In addition to hearing prophecy and seeing visions, other provocative examples include: dream visitations, demonic release, and the power to experience God praying for you (a much misunderstood ability known as "praying in tongues"—explained later), as well as forms of healing (physical, emotional, intellectual, etc.)

Those experiences aren't our focus here, but they should be mentioned just to put prophecy on the map.

We are offered a copious variety of benefits.

Are all these charisms listed in the Bible?

Most of them are, but the Bible says that not everything is written about in the accounts. [John 21:25] But the regular ones are. And of course, if everything divine act had to be chronicled that would eliminate many loving expressions.

We need to be careful not to limit Father God on what presents he wants to give us, especially by pre-judging the packaging.

Where are these gifts being opened today?

The worldwide trend for experiencing these "two-way" encounters, and is generally referred to as the Charismatic movement. It's apparently the fastest growing wave in humanity, with reports of 600–700 million participants, and the most fantastic surge in this past century.

It's on the increase. Something immense is happening all over, right now.

Why so much growth this past century?

Historically, two explosive outpourings of manifestations have occurred: in the early church centuries, but even more so in our age. There have been more reported miracles in Christianity within the past century than in all other centuries combined. And that's not just by volume, but by percentage.

To explain, some refer to a prediction in the Bible [Acts 2:17-21] that the outpouring of God will be as the spring and autumn rains in Israel: water for planting and water for harvest. The implication seems to be that we live in the last scene of mankind's story. Jesus said to read general clues, but that we won't know precise dates, [Matt 24:36] so no one can say exactly how long our last chapter will be. Whatever theology we use, the global trends continue strong.

In the modern West, because religions often lean toward abstract, impersonal principles, rather than concrete, organic, relationships, we might falsely assume God's gift-giving over time must be uniformly, linearly distributed. However, that doesn't seem to be the biblical way. Unpredictable patterns make better sense, and are more natural.

For example, in film narratives, a natural story arc usually consists of three acts: an early attention-getter that generates interest, intermediate character development to deepen investment, and finally an enhanced action climax. It looks like we're somewhere in Act III.

How does the charismatic movement fit into Christianity?

Statistically, the movement currently already comprises 25% of Christianity, within existing denominations (Evangelical, Orthodox, Protestant, Roman Catholic, etc.), but it's most certainly active in groups expecting charisms, such as charismatic and Pentecostal churches, where Christianity grows much more rapidly.

But don't let names deprive you of your God-given gifts. There is a lot of blurring.

For instance, for our purposes "charismatic" and "Pentecostal" are synonymous, though there are some differences in history and approach. The name Pentecostal refers to the inaugural Holy Spirit miracle-fest, which took place as Jesus promised, literally "50 days" after Easter.

It's more helpful to view the charisms as energy boosters in the supernatural dimension throughout Christianity, rather than a separate compartment within the church. The wine goes with the whole meal.

Because these experiences are life-changing, bringing more color and energy, the renewal can somehow appear as a separate version of Christianity, but it's more like blossoms on a flower; or perhaps like being in love with someone and then receiving a kiss. Afterward, you're different.

How does the Bible talk about prophecy?

Technically, the Bible itself exists as a massive, unique prophecy—a love letter from God, through one nation to all.

Paul instructs us to follow love and crave the greater charisms, especially prophecy, because it's a supreme motivator. [I Cor 14:1] He loved this gift, saying, "I wish you would all prophesy."

He explains prophecy's purpose as edification, exhortation, and consolation; (or as the saying goes, to "build up, stir up, and cheer up").

Who has this gift?

Everyone hears God already. Two obvious sources that Paul cites are from conscience and creation (inside us and outside us). [Rom 1:20]

So broadly speaking, everyone has some ability to hear God. However, "prophecy" usually refers to a more amplified revelation.

Does prophecy mean predicting the future?

Pope Francis nicely blended the present and future aspects during a Christmas message (the gift-giving season): "A prophet is someone who listens to the words of God, who reads the spirit of the times, and who knows how to move forward towards the future."

It's a shame the word "prophecy" gets hijacked to mean only predictions; but the Greek word for "prophet" means "mouth," or "one who speaks as another."

But doesn't prophecy include predictions?

Yes, but in the Bible, and in modern prophecy, most messages are for the present time, although many are certainly forecasts.

The world's most famous prophesier, Jesus, forecasted that we would prophesy too—and in even greater ways—because he's doing it today *through* us.

(Imagine Jesus trying to do his ministry without prophecy.)

Does modern prophecy add to the completed Bible?

Never. Think of the Bible as public, settled revelation; and modern messages as private, ongoing revelation. What we now receive simply illuminates a particular part of the Bible that is needed for a present situation.

If that's not the case, then any leading from God could be accused of adding to the Bible.

Also note that there were prophesiers referenced in the Bible whose unrecorded content was considered valid, yet their words are not found in the Bible.

Here's a better way to look at it: The Bible is like Father God speaking to all of his kids saying he'll be visiting each one to speak with them personally.

That's more accurate.

Where is this in the Bible?

It's actually the main point of the New Testament: God is no longer "out there" but "in here."

Jesus said to wait for the Holy Spirit power experience at Pentecost and from then on his life would impregnate humanity corporately. And boom—Christianity has grown just as he prophetically predicted, from the smallest seed to the largest, global, spiritual family tree. [Matt 13:32]

So Jesus is actually still alive, corporately, in those who love him?

I didn't make this up, but that's what the people who are apparently closest to him are enjoying, pretty much completely unorchestrated by anyone on earth. Mystically, we are like cells in his Body.

Christianity arrived primarily via the West, through which God gave thus us enormous gifts, such as the amplification of human rights, science, reason, various arts, and most obviously the supernatural experience of Christ—all designed to be given away to everyone else.

And that happened! Christianity is currently much more internationally popular in the non-West. For instance, there are now roughly as many Christians in China as in the United States (around 160 million).

So what happened to Christianity in the West?

Here's my speculation of two possible causes for its decline (one healthy and one unhealthy).

Explanation 1: As the tree grew, some places simply now have more bark than sap. It's just part of the natural lifecycle.

Explanation 2: Jesus said it's difficult for those with temporary wealth (e.g., money, health, talent, entertainment, resources, intelligence, technology) to detach in favor of the permanent wealth of the Kingdom. [Luke 18:25] It's likely that these formidable addictions obscure our deeper need.

In either case, Jesus today continues to reverse the crazy deception that God is most concerned with things over people, formulas over Fathering, rules over relationships, principles over persons, the letter the law over the Spirit of the law, etc.

The modern West sometimes doesn't see that.

Because we value abstract principles so much, we can even blunder into thinking the Bible actually takes primacy over Jesus. But it doesn't. The Bible is his word.

Here is an insight that helped me. There are two New Testament Greek words that both translate into the English term for "word":

"logos" (eternal, unchanging revelation to all); and "rhema" (timely, changeable revelation to individuals)

Modern prophecy is "rhema."

Why haven't we heard that explanation of "word" before?

Perhaps we've been overexposed to environments emphasizing God speaking generally, but not specifically.

Is there an easy way to remember this?

Here's a quick summary. Individual private revelation can't substitute for biblical public revelation; but neither can biblical public revelation substitute for individual private revelation.

Derek Prince gives this picture: The Bible is like a piano, and the Holy Spirit is the piano player. To hear music, we need both.

(Sorry for the extra detail here, but major stumbling blocks can exist for some whose religious environments don't expect much. When deprived of encounters, we might substitute innermost needs with doctrines or with someone else's encounter. Thanks for your patience clearing these obstacles.)

Doesn't the Old Testament tell us to punish the inaccurate prophet?

This again is a common question from certain religious mindsets.

The answer is evident with the right basic view of the Old versus the New Testament, so let's take a few questions to explore that difference, especially since it deals with how God sees us today.

There is a chastising verse for that in the Torah as a means of purifying that prominent office. However, we don't live under the Old Testament covenant today, but under the New Testament covenant.

You're saying we tend to think of prophets in an Old Testament way?

Definitely. The model then was of one prophet to many people, whereas the new covenant is that now everyone gets to prophesy.

(There's more on this upcoming in part 3.2.)

So what is the distinction between Old and New Testament related to the gift of prophecy?

We get an upgrade: the Old Testament focused on discerning the *prophet*; but the New Testament emphasizes discerning the *prophecy*.

This has huge relevance because if we assume God is just "out there" and not "in here," that lowers our expectations because we think we have to qualify.

So there's a big difference.

Old Testament prophets mainly call out the bad; New Testament prophets mainly call out the good.

The Old Testament is a sin x-ray, but the New Testament is a blueprint for inheritance.

Therefore any Spirit-filled person today should see Christ in you and be declaring that life manifest in you "on earth as it is in Heaven."

Wow. that's a way different perspective than just following the rules.

The amazing point of the New Testament is that anyone can accept God's self-gift.

That's exactly what the cross and resurrection are all about—the centerpiece and masterpiece of our realm.

God gave himself to us and anyone can give themselves to God.

But don't we need doctrines, laws, and principles?

Rules are like the white lines on a football field. We need them, but Jesus is more interested in helping us score touchdowns.

That's a relief. So it's O.K. to be partly correct when prophesying?

Paul says "we prophesy in part." [I Cor 13:9]

Mistakes must be allowed, because otherwise we would be required to be 100% virtuous, which is obviously impossible.

The key here is that our identity is not based on our obedience, accuracy, mood or on anything else but the reality of God's gift of himself.

If there can be mistakes, then how do we know true prophets and true prophecy?

Stay tuned for more on discernment later in part 3.6.

For that we first need more personal experience.

3.1—PERSONAL MESSAGES

So today we can hear God speaking personally to us, even word-for-word?

Yes, and it's more widespread than sometimes realized.

Let's continue straight in, so we can experience more ourselves. There's nothing more convincing than that.

During my initial exposure to prophecy, I was skeptical. Many years ago, a trusted gentleman I met in college told me he had received pages of letters from God, which shocked me, and precipitated an avalanche of tough questions. But I couldn't find any fault in his arguments, and he was also a high quality friend.

I later heard others in prayer groups receiving prophecies. I was again very suspicious (being a Type A, modern American, Alpha male), so I asked them to pray for specific requests *independently*—and was amazed how frequently they received either the same message, or something so close that I suspected collusion. Yet there wasn't any. This correlation still continues in my life.

With the right heart, God invites this type of testing, as our good Father. He wants to deliver. [Luke 12:32]

So start with what you can trust about God and then move into more challenging areas.

(I'm not done exploring this either!)

I'm still a little uncomfortable with another person speaking as if they were Jesus.

That's an understandable emotional obstacle, especially if we were implicitly taught that Christ is only outside of us, and not alive inside.

Somehow we miss Christ within, yet may also wonder why we don't get more manifestations. But these two issues connect. So watch for the hidden false assumption of "God lives only outside me."

By the way, prophets in the Bible, church history and today never say they are actually Jesus.

So God's life shines through us?

That's a good way to see it: Jesus speaking through us is as light through stained glass.

What if I'm not yet convinced that I need to give or receive prophecies? I'm fine with just knowing the Bible.

Not everything that Jesus wants for you is recorded in the Bible. [John 16:13]

Personally, I never understood why we wouldn't want Jesus speaking more to us. What an advantage that is.

What are some reasons we hide behind to avoid hearing God?

Two rationalizations are that prophecy is either:

1) unreal, imaginary fluff (only from you), or
2) real, dangerous stuff (from the devil).

Could modern messages be from an evil spirit?

Of course; that's why the Bible tells us to check for counterfeits.

In my experience it would be difficult to conclude the bulk of the messages are from demons because they consistently promote uncomplicated surrender to Christ, worship, holiness, love, joy, repentance, healing, unity, miracles, freedom, service, etc. (Why would the enemy promote the highest things?)

Why think that the devil speaks clear temptations, yet Father God doesn't speak clear blessings? That's twisted.

Here's a clue: watch for soiled negativity toward God's gifts, such thinking that as even if they're real, they're not desirable.

Beware of this self-contradiction: "Modern prophecy doesn't exist! Thus saith the Lord." Hmmm.

You mean, beware of buzzkillers?

Any party-pooper implying that "God is not speaking to you—and he's not speaking to anybody" might be a red flag. It's as if that person is saying, "Your party is a violation, and so are all parties"—even though Jesus promised them.

Any negative voice might be taking itself too seriously, and God's mercy not seriously enough.

But didn't Jesus say, "Beware of false prophets"?

Yes, but he didn't say, "Beware of prophets"!

I like Kris Vallotton's sensible comments that false prophets imply the existence of true prophets. It's not that "in the last days all the prophets will be false." (So rather, beware of *no* prophets.)

Shouldn't we be cautious?

Even when so, that doesn't mean default to hesitation, doubt, skepticism, disbelief, etc. Love is our baseline.

What if I've been burned by supposed prophetic messages?

Sorry—that's always painful. Really. But see below, part 3.5 on Battle Strategies and *Wounding*. Big topic.

The enemy throws in toxic side dishes so that we won't consume anything, though we still need to eat.

You're saying we can't avoid dealing with the supernatural?

We publicly default to the non-supernatural. Obviously, when it comes to God, we need both natural and supernatural.

Hence, when there's cultural tension, will we invest in Heaven? These issues comprise our primary drama. When the mob hates Jesus, where will I side?

Love always has risk.

Therefore the God of Love does too. But we risk far more by not proactively trusting him.

For example, Pope Francis says, "I would rather have a Church that makes mistakes for doing something, than one that gets sick for being closed up."

Bill Johnson also says "I would rather that we error on the side of excess, than of lack."

What does this mean practically?

One thing it means is rejecting the bizarre tendency to have more faith that God is not speaking than that he is.

Also, in the Bible, prophetic supernatural experiences often arrive upfront, because they give us radar on our life's position, which gives us actionable intelligence.

For example, the bourgeoning movements for effective healing prayer are so influential today because the gifts matured in prior decades. It's much harder to release deep inner trauma without prophetic light.

Does God have particular promises for me?

Absolutely. *Tangible* promises are given to help survive times of trial, since that builds trust. This theme is all over the Bible.

So a good question is "What are the specific promises God has made to me?"

For example, Paul reminded his young apprentice: "Timothy, my son, I am giving you this command in keeping with the prophecies once made about you, so that by recalling them you may fight the battle well." [I Ti 1:18]

The word is a seed [Luke 8:11] with the DNA already present within. It grows by itself. [Mark 4:27]

The underlying idea behind the promises is that God's words and actions match. He has *integritas*— wholeness, faithfulness, completeness. Receiving a word and watching its fulfillment bonds us together.

Also, we might forget Jesus had to live completely off of the Father's promises.

So we just sit around and wait for God's promises to be fulfilled?

No. It requires an active receptivity, like preparing soil just because God told you rain is coming.

For instance, if a word from God says you will go to grad school, then apply around.

Can anyone be a prophet? Can anyone get a prophetic word?

Great questions. To explore them, we're going to need to make some distinctions between a prophet and prophecy.

3.2—Prophets and Prophecy

Does a person need to be a committed Christian to have the gift of prophecy?

Actually no, according to Jesus. [Matt 7:21] Not all who have prophecy are close to him. (This fits the fact that everyone has some version of the gift to begin with, as we mentioned earlier.)

But to be a bona fide *Christian,* then a person must commit their heart to Christ, and this is infinitely more important than any prophetic word.

Non-Christians might do this anonymously, but with less awareness for Christ's immediate presence. For example, Jesus commends the Queen of Sheba as one of his own [Matt 12:42]. So a reader of this book who wouldn't label themselves Christian might already be implicitly committed to Christ, but it's always better to make that explicit.

What we think God requires is often confused. It's not how much you know, feel, do, serve, give, prophesy, or attend. The issue is whether a person gives their heart/center/I/spirit/self, based on whatever revelation God has provided.

At it's core, Christianity is a marriage, a covenant commitment that exchanges lives, however aware we are of that reality. (And no one is totally aware of it!)

So anyone can exercise prophecy, not just prophets?

All believers have a prophetic gift; but not all are "prophets." [I Cor 12:29]

So what's the difference between prophet and prophecy?

A prophet is one who has prophecy as their first gift. You could call it having a prophetic temperament.

Just as with personality temperaments (e.g., Myers-Briggs), everyone has all the character qualities, but each person specializes. For instance, everyone has feelings, but some are more fluid with them.

Here's another illustration: every one has a set of binoculars, but some use them as their primary device.

I don't want this to be confusing.

Agreed. Not to worry. The labels aren't the main thing.

The big reason to distinguish between prophets and prophecy is to avoid bad conclusions that block God's gifts, such as "My prophetic ability isn't dramatic, so I'm not close to God".

My friends with strong gifts used to debate me on this issue, because I would claim that I didn't have their flashy powers, such as seeing angels. Yet God would often speak to them through me. So they would say, "You're a prophet!" and then I would quip: "No I'm not—and I got a prophetic word that said so."

It turns out we were both half-right, given the distinctions above. Like everyone, I have a prophetic dimension; but in my case it's not my primary, go-to gift.

Do I have a prophetic temperament?

If your spiritual temperament is not already known, then it will be made evident over time. Like rose bushes and oak trees that grow more glorious with nourishment, whatever is already in your DNA will eventually declare its nature.

Spiritual temperaments might include those listed in Romans 12:6–8 (sometimes called "redemptive gifts"): Prophet, Servant, Teacher, Encourager, Giver, Ruler, Mercy.

But that's another topic. We don't have to worry about it. Your temperament will become clear.

"Prophet" and "prophecy" are used ambiguously.

True.

Two ways that we can err, is either by saying "everyone is a prophet" or by saying "I don't get prophecy."

For this publication, we can just simplify to make it easier and use the terms synonymously.

The main thing is not to limit yourself with labels. We're trying to encourage everyone to hear God's voice.

If everyone can prophecy, who are the prophets?

That's determined by God, by the person and by the church—not just by the person. In fact, watch out for self-proclaimed prophets!—and I'm not one. ;)

So the church-at-large plays a role?

An individual prophet supports the group and the group supports the individual prophet.

Therefore be wary of prophets who work in isolation. That doesn't mean they are necessarily bad-hearted, but they will always be more vulnerable to self-deception.

As a pivotal leader in the Roman Catholic charismatic renewal, Fr. Cantalamessa (the one-and-only preacher to the Pope for about 35 years) said all pastors must cultivate parish supernatural charisms and *must not fear* experiencing the Holy Spirit.

Pastors are like gardeners, and prophets like fragile flowers, easily trampled. Authority must be a protective roof.

So both leaders and prophets benefit.

Rulers and prophets team, like King David and his gifted bro Nathan.

Prophets need to forgive the church when they've been rejected, and church leaders need to repent of squelching prophecy. Paul says don't despise it and thus quench the Holy Spirit's fire. [I Thes 5:20]

It seems more frequent that leadership squelches supernatural leadings.

That's true. Authority wields a disproportionate consequence. That's probably one reason why Jesus taught to lead by submission as a safeguard. [John 13:14]

Pope Francis is a good role model for this, who said: "When there is no spirit of prophecy among the people of God, we fall into the trap of clericalism… when clericalism reigns supreme the words of God are sorely missed, and true believers weep because they cannot find the Lord."

Clericalism, a rampant problem, is the overpromotion of leadership—especially when the leader's voice tries to displace God's in your heart. That's a big no-no.

But when authority is defective, should I still submit?

Certainly there needs to be a discernment when a prophet should leave abusive authority, but not having any authority is just exchanging one bad situation for temporary survival. It's like leaving a sailing vessel in an escape pod because of a psychotic Captain. Neither situation is ideal.

By the way, speaking of larger groups, it's not just individuals who have spiritual temperaments, but families, cities and nations. Can you guess which temperament America is?

The United States is a prophet nation?

This notion (which I think I first heard from Arthur Burk) is very interesting when we consider typical prophet characteristics. For example:

-- America separated from oppressive authority to herald individualism, rights, and freedom.

-- We're less interested in permanent physical conquest, preferring idea-warfare. (But then we try to make other nations prophets too, even out of ones that aren't supposed to be!)

-- We "see" things ahead of time, which is an ability that can be used for spiritual or material increase. But despite being the richest nation ever, we're not the happiest. For all our strengths, we can be like a spoiled only child.

Are you saying America is dysfunctional?

Well, yes and no. But that's a tangential issue.

In brief, America is like an exceptionally gifted person with both virtues and vices.

But the point here is that being prophetic, our American challenge is that culture implicitly trains us to isolate. We need to work to overcome that.

So, if you are considered a prophet, stay plugged in. The Body is your protection. And if you are in authority, protect your prophets.

So leadership should be helping me cultivate my prophetic gift?

Yes. And as you unpack your gifts, you can help release others.

But keep in mind, these powers aren't always fully developed—hence this media effort. Paul coaches us to "Fan into flame the gift given to you during the laying on of hands prayer." [2 Tim 1:6]

If we are not hearing God directly, is something wrong?

Not necessarily. There are times of quiet and times of wordless activity.

On any particular day, not hearing doesn't mean anything by itself. We sometimes need more info. God could be chilaxing.

However, in general, hearing is normal, just as with any healthy marriage. The overarching issue is always "How is the relationship?"

Do you mean hearing is normal because love is normal?

If God is Love, then we naturally encounter God in various ways.

Let's move more into those specifics.

"Taste and see." [Psalm 34:8]

3.3—EXPERIENCING PROPHECY

How can I receive more if I'm still having trouble believing these are supernatural messages?

God understands that. So he helps build our confidence by giving us circumstantial confirmations.

Here's a story to illustrate. At my friend's house, she served me a fine dinner, and then provided a dessert loaded with strawberries. I don't dislike them, but almost never eat them, yet on this occasion decided to indulge all of them. (It felt like I probably ate more that night than in the rest of my life combined.) Anyway, on the way home I was praying on the phone with another marvelously gifted friend who had a motivating, but basic, vision for me and then said to me, "And I have no idea what this means—maybe you might—but the Lord is asking you: *'What is it about you and strawberries?!'*" My friend had no clue about what had just happened. (Further, she has been spectacularly accurate on numerous occasions, down to astonishing details.)

To expand this point even further: I am very good friends with about twenty, top-tier, talented prophets, and have coached several dozen more with testable gifts. And I'm just one person in the grand mix. It's available. Jesus said "Seek and you will discover." [Matt 7:7]

I could provide more fun stories, but let's leave it there.

Why would God address trivial things like strawberries?

First, God talks to us about everything. If it's on your heart, then the Father cares—even more than you do. [Luke 12:7]

Second, the preceding vision she had was relevant to me, and I might have dismissed it because there was nothing externally verifiable about it. So sometimes the more impressive, information-rich confirmations help reinforce the less confirmable, but often more important revelations. That is, over and over God says he loves us and confirms it.

Third, certainly God relates to both the most serious and most silly; but I tell this stories because it's approachable, real, and non-threatening.

God will converse about anything?

Anything. But note that his words are often directional and require a response, like a parent to a child.

When my mother was in the Sunrise assisted-living residence before she went home to the Lord, I used to print out for her some of these messages to help inspire her in letting go and trusting God. But one day she read a message that contained the phrase "The Kingdom of God is not 'Burger King'—'Have it Your Way'". My seasoned Irish mother then boldly proclaimed "This could not possibly be inspired! God does not talk about things like Burger King."

I'm sure Jesus laughed. (In fact, after Easter Jesus and the disciples had broiled fish "burgers.") And to be fair to Burger King, it's just a typical advertiser expression, trying to tap our needs.

You can read that prophetic passage, in the Section One messages, ironically titled "Let Go."

Letting go seems to be a main theme in our lives.

We're basically all babies. We just need to believe, behave, and be.

Generally, any time we let go of a lesser good to receive a greater good, we take a risk that the Father has more provision. That's how we are weaned into trust.

We have to release the grip on yesterday to receive the future. Jesus used the image of discarding old wine carriers to obtain the better wine. [Mark 2:22]

Does the cover of this book suggest that Christ a wine lover?

I didn't make this up: Jesus represents himself with bread (sustenance) and wine (abundance).

Aren't you presenting Jesus as a little too casual?

Well, he's not only casual. He's both formal and informal, but we're typically used to relating more formally. C.S. Lewis memorably united both in the famous phrase "Joy is the serious business of Heaven."

To get close to us, God has to access our center. The formal is outer and the informal is inner, hence the emphasis.

The wedding ceremony is formal; the honeymoon isn't.

So you're accenting the intimacy of God.

God can't be any more in love with us than water can be more wet. Years ago, this was one of the first things he spoke to me: "You know the feeling you have when you're drunk in love with someone? I feel that way about you all the time."

Awesome. That's a big incentive for hearing God.

Motivations are more important than the mechanics. That's what I'm trying to emphasize here.

Although, we need both.

Specifically, what does it feel like to hear God speak?

Impressions range from indirect to direct, and from vague to vivid.

One helpful tip: The messages often have the nature of your own thoughts, yet don't sound like you *originated* them. You are "spoken to." It feels as if someone else were speaking in your heart—because that's exactly what's happening.

Interestingly, you don't even have to be fully alert to get a clear word. I developed a friendship with Francis J. Roberts, author of *Come Away My Beloved,* and she told me that most of the messages she received were when she was awakened by the Spirit at 2 a.m. Then rising again at daybreak and reading them was as big a shock to her as anyone.

I like Graham Cooke's comment about his prophetic teaching materials, which he jokingly calls "the best books I never wrote."

We all know the answer deep down. We can hear God better than we think. It's the same as connecting with your conscience, except more pronounced, more varied, and more colorful.

Describe more about being "spoken to"?

It has a sense of surprise. The thought arrives without your initiation, having the same unpredictability as in a dialogue with any person.

Many also report a special "sizzle" on the correspondence, as if the words jump off the page. They have a certain highlight, resonance, sweetening, life, energy, moxie, spice, or sparkle. In essence, somehow the thoughts are more *alive*.

Even when this communication is subtle, it's somehow still there?

Correct. But note that candidates for vital revelation are testable, otherwise why would God instruct us to test?

Must God speak to us in first-person?

Not at all. But in cases where the messages are more obvious, that's not infrequent.

The arrival of words in first-person is secondary. For instance, a wordless JPEG photo can be more captivating than a text message, or vice versa. It depends on the love present within.

Are you saying the medium is not important?

No, just that the message is more important than the medium; the content over the container, the meaning over the letters. [2 Cor 3:6]

How else can we discern the message?

Augustine gives us this tip: the mind can change the interpretation, but not the message itself.

It's similar to reading the Bible, there's content and commentary.

(Unlike our private revelations, the Bible's content has already been tested by the church-at-large.)

So we might be more certain of one part of the message more than another?

I like to ask the receiver, "What part are you more confident was from the Holy Spirit, and what part was more just from you?"

This is especially helpful if the word contains directive action.

Anything important is best confirmed by at least few prophets on a few occasions, if needed.

Revelations progressively unfold?

Many of my friends gifts' developed over the years. Often they start out as more blurry. Part of this advancement can attributed to the visions becoming clearer, and part can be due to the person learning to lean in closer to God.

I am not saying that God's voice necessarily gets louder, but that we learn to recognize it better, and the net effect is hearing more clearly.

So the gift *grows*?

The gift is organic because relationships are organic.

Jesus mainly taught via living analogies.

Sometimes the vision itself can be gradual. One friend of ours, who has probably received several hundred by now, says sometimes they "beam in" like the Star Trek transporter materialization special effect. As Paul says, we see through a refracted glass. [I Cor 13:12]

There can definitely be a mystery aspect to prophecy. Someone once described it as "having a photographic memory of something you've never seen."

So prophecy is always obscure?

No: mysteries are partly sunny, partly cloudy.

For example, on one occasion, God gave a friend of mine a clear vision of me watching a very expensive HDTV, but the program was all blurry digital pixelization! The humor in this was that Jesus was instructing me to not strain my eyes—he would flip on the program at the scheduled time.

The example above illustrates the distinction between medium and message.

Sometimes it's a clear picture, but you don't understand it; or it's a fuzzy picture, yet you know exactly what it means!

Does God tease us?

Only for fun. ;)

Sometimes it's just part of helping us grow up.

But it's not all comedy.

Certainly not. But Father God is a good parent, playful and practical. He loves to enrich life.

For instance, I'm fascinated by how prophetic words proclaim central teaching we've heard repeatedly, yet at the same time they remain fresh. Like the messages in this book, God uses popularly quoted biblical material, but never generates religious clichés. The gum never loses its flavor.

In the end, somehow you just know when a word is from God?

It's exactly like becoming familiar with a friend's voice, but this case the voice is speaking within you.

In one sense it's fair to answer "You just know it" because that's how we know most elementary things: consciousness, conscience, experiencing beauty, free will, reasoning, falling in love, any pleasure or any pain. Fundamental sense experience is, of course, how we primarily perceive all of life.

If you have a spirit, then you have a spiritual sense.

So sense more with the spirit than with the mind.

Paul says that "Spiritual things are discerned by the spirit, not by the wisdom of man." [1 Cor 2:14]

Somehow that verse used to confuse me, but turns out to be so simple! Lovers know love.

3.4—ATMOSPHERES

For this part, I'd like to build on the notion that impressions you receive are not always distinct. In other words, love can have a certain spirit or atmosphere.

How do we detect this? Simple awareness?

Yes. It's kind of like paying attention to the "weather" of the relationship.

How does this help us distinguish God's voice?

The presence of God has a certain Shalom, or satisfaction. It will not have a gloomy, overcast feel to it, even when we're chastised.

If we don't feel sunshine, it doesn't mean God isn't involved. But if we sense oppression, we can first invite God into it before acting.

For example, notice how your thoughts can be from yourself, God, or the enemy, who will tempt via disguised first person comments such as, "I'll never make it." That may or may not be your thought!

The resulting cloud of discouragement can help us back track to the source.

Why do spirits live in the mist? Why wouldn't God just be clearer?

It turns out we're the ones in the mist.

There can be various reasons for this:

Sometimes we're just not there yet.
Sometimes God wants clarity, but we don't ask for it.
Sometimes details are veiled to enhance anticipation.
Sometimes he is clear, but we deny the message.
Sometimes our trust needs reinforcing.
Sometimes God enjoys asking questions of us too.

So it depends.

Usually it's just because we are kids growing up, into greater awareness of the Father.

Then these messages are not primarily about information.

We can delete the idea that the purpose of prophecy is to give us enough knowledge so we won't need God!

But what if I get a message and I'm not sure of the meaning?

Ask for clarification, as you would when talking to anyone. If we believe responses are rare, we won't think to ask.

The dynamic in the Gospels is that the best rewards were often given to those who bartered with Jesus. He enjoys your company.

The messages in this book don't cover all the teachings in the Gospel. Why not?

This very common question is a peculiar misunderstanding that any revelation from God must completely replicate the Bible as if his main mission is to offer a comprehensive discourse on doctrine, rather than to be with the person.

So the messages in this book are definitely not a Scripture rewrite, but part of the promised biblical stimulus package.

Jesus customizes interactions. He doesn't recount every biblical theme each time he speaks.

So if Christ relates to each in a customized way, then each person must color the messages?

Yeah, and that's *good*. We are all unique, artistic, hand-tinted windows for God's glory.

Where things get complicated is when the glass has dirt (sin) or cracks (wounds).

Coloring flavors, but dirt and cracks distort.

And dirt is much easier to remove if the cracks are repaired, and vice versa.

What is this book's color like?

Let's compare it to two other authors: Sarah Young's messages are more timely, individual, gentle. Francis J. Roberts' are more timeless, epic, weighty. My friend's synthesis seems to be somewhere in-between.

Like a good wine that is both firm and fruitful, good prophetic words a nice blend of both hard and soft, tough and tender, cross and resurrection, real and ideal, literal and analogical, local and global, etc.

For example, I noticed that two phrases in these messages that kept recurring were "surrendering" and "abundance," hence the book's title.

Can you offer suggestions for how to review these messages?

Read with God, listening for what he wants to emphasize.

Read slowly. Many of these prophecies arrived over years, some soaked in hours of worship sessions. If we go too fast, blasting through like data scavengers, we'll miss absorption, and then transformation. Jesus described superficiality as a seed falling on shallow ground. [Mark 4:5]

Because the writings are like chunks of dense chocolate, if you read them all at once they will be too rich to process. Perhaps just savor one and ask God what's relevant to you.

Fortunately, the messages are general enough to appeal to anyone, yet specific enough to speak right to you. God expertly integrates the universal and unique.

Certain parts will apply to us and other parts to others?

Definitely. God speaks to my friend in this book primarily based on what he needs, which may not be what we need.

For example, his personality temperament is a phlegmatic type (INFP), and they tend to be laid-back, gentle, bridge-building souls, that occasionally need a good dose of discipline to reach their goals. (Note: I'm ESTJ, the opposite, which you can hear in the interview.)

However, it is timely for his collection to be available now, because our current millennial society specializes in phlegmatic gifts! Previous generations seemed to go through seasons that blurred into each other, such as melancholic (1945–1965), choleric (1965–1977), sanguine (1977–1999), etc.

So these words have a certain slant?

Everyone's words do. That's another reason to notice atmospheres.

When a message seems to carry a special sense that it's from God, you might say you can "smell the anointing" about it.

What do you mean we can smell the anointing?

That's just slang for experiencing in your spirit whether something has God's special approval on it.

People, groups, places, times, events, music, films, sports, etc., all can have this spiritual weather about them. It's an overall sense of delight vs. oppression, satisfaction or strife, sunlight or darkness.

How do we detect spiritual atmospheres?

Here's a simple example from football:

Commentators talk about how the game's "momentum" has shifted and a team's energy is up or down.

Interestingly, statisticians collect every imaginable trivia—except that momentum mojo—and yet that aspect is always reported on in every game. How are announcers, fans, coaches, and players picking this up? With their spirits.

It's like when a band at a concert seems to be coming together with that special synergy.

It's easy to know, so we just need to pay attention.

It's mostly just listening to what your spirit is already perceiving.

What do you mean by "mojo"?

It's just another way to say atmosphere, energy, flow, tone, impression—one of the properties when we mean something has good spirit.

Good mojo is the intuitive vibe that love has. It's like the famous Beatles line "something in the way she moves me."

Notice Jesus said that he was that very quality: the Way. [John 14:6] And early on, the church wasn't known as Christianity, but was called "The Way." It's not merely directional.

So we should consider not just what is said, but the *way* it's said?

Yes, this is essential because the way we speak, by emphasis, can change the truth *meaning*.

For example, the phrase "I love you" can have opposite meanings depending on different audio inflections, including something as fundamental as whether it's a statement or question. "I *love* you" vs. "I love *you*?"

Without thinking, we intuitively perceive the attributes, such as syntax, timing, tone, impression, etc.

To give another example, if we prophetically announce someone's wrongdoing, but do it in a judgmental, unloving tone, the effect may not motivate that person to change, but to leave.

So we need to develop the habit of reading in-between the lines.

In a movie, the implied meaning within the unspoken dialogue is called the subtext. It's just as important as the spoken text. So be aware of what is *not* said.

For example, reject any prophecy given to you that accurately critiques, but offers no exit. "God is faithful; he will not let you be tempted beyond what you can bear. But when you are tempted, he will also provide a way out so that you can endure it." [I Cor 10:13] Why? Because "Love never fails." [I Cor 13:8]

In these dead-end condemnations you are rightly diagnosed as having a problem, but there is no solution. It's judgment without mercy, a cheeseless maze.

When you sense the darkness, don't receive the word.

You've talked about atmospheres, anointings, and mojos—why use all these strange terms?

Because we live in a world predominated by digital technology, and so we're too used to expecting God to show up via a calculated technique. If God is love, and love is unquantifiable, then we need to use our unquantifiable senses.

And I find that these are things everyone already knows instinctively anyway. We just need reminders.

God loves engagement. When we respond with more expectation, the relationship develops a more pleasant, interactive flavor.

That's great news. But why is it so challenging?

In this world we get beaten up, and that's no small factor.

3.5—BATTLE STRATEGIES AND WOUNDING

O.K., now we come to the gritty discussion of spiritual combat.

We all have hurts in life from conflicts, and those pains distort our perspective. Famous heavyweight boxing champion Mike Tyson said, "Everyone has a plan, until they get punched in the mouth."

If prophets receive from God, they will get hit with some form of a spiritual beating?

Correct. And not only do they get attacked, but they are usually the *first* ones to get attacked.

Why is our prophetic channel attacked first?

Because the prayer connection is like the Internet to God. That's why Paul says to seek prophecy early, to help secure comms.

For instance, during war, an attacking country initiates a first strike by disabling their enemy's GPS.

Prophets get attacked first. That's terrible.

Yeah, but it gets worse: Satan best accomplishes this from *within* the church!

Jesus refers to this notion when he says that "a prophet receives honor everywhere but in his family and home town." [Luke 4:24]

Remember that Jesus' betrayal began with one of his closest friends.

That's painful—Christians attacking each other and thinking they're doing God's will.

It's most agonizing to Christ—suffering a torn body.

In medicine, when one good body part attacks another, it's called an autoimmune disease. Christendom is infected with this right now, whether between Catholics and Protestants, within those groups, within families, within thy very self.

But there's exciting news: right now Christ is miraculously healing divisions via the unifying presence of the Holy Spirit. This is not mere theory. It's been happening big time all over the world.

Cardinal Bergoglio, before he became Pope Francis, had responsibility for the charismatic renewal and participated in this wave in Argentina, receiving laying on of hands prayer from Catholics and Protestants.

How are prophets rejected?

Usually via social trauma. Jesus said he had "no place to rest his head." [Luke 9:58]

Deep wounds would certainly damage a prophet.

Yes, so we must all be careful not to base our identity on others' reactions.

Beware of something called a legitimacy curse, which in the case of a prophet means "If you reject the prophecy, then you reject the prophet." That's a lie. A prophet is God's child.

So be tender with prophets if you want their contribution!

What struggles are typical for prophets?

Discouraging, subtle thoughts often arrive in first-person, such as: "I know I'm hearing from God, but no one understands me" or "Since I experience these things, I'm closer to God than everyone else" or "I can't trust anyone because they'll never get me."

Wouldn't wounds result in jaded messages?

Bingo. A prophet easily develops emotional wounds, followed by sins, which will distort prophetic light.

C.S. Lewis says, "The instrument through which you see God is your whole self. And if a man's self is not kept clean and bright, his glimpse of God will be blurred—like the moon seen through a dirty telescope."

So a pure person has purer vision?

Jesus says if you want to see God, have a pure heart. [Matt 5:8]

Purity isn't puritanical, but rather an un-cracked lens, a reliable will, an undivided heart. Because perfect purity is unattainable, then the practical take here is that a person with a good heart will more freely check in with God for corrections.

Notice a person with a good spirit will discern better than a person with a big gift because prophecy is merely a *magnifier* of the spirit.

For instance, it's better to see dimly in the right direction, than see well in the wrong direction.

So a wound such as a bruised emotion might impel us to prophesy selfishly?

Right.

Therefore we need to make a meaningful distinction. Hopefully this won't be confusing.

The expressions "false prophet" and "bad prophet" can be ambiguous, because both are sometimes used to mean either evil or inaccurate. However, inaccurate prophecy may or may not be evil, but evil prophecy always intends to harm you, even when accurate.

So when those terms are used, try to figure out which is meant.

If wounding is such an issue, how can we help?

Beyond asking God for connection protection, we can recognize that the Lord strategically places prophets where they can see, like the crewmembers stationed way up in the crow's nest of a sailing vessel. The same quality that allows them to see, makes them accessible to enemy fire.

It can seem as if prophets are somehow on the "outside," of but they aren't.

So accessibility requires protection?

Yes, because not only can wounds distort messages, but they can damage persons.

For instance, if we take in a bad word and then end up shutting down all prophecy, that's tragic.

So note here that wounds can exist with the giver or the receiver. It's about what comes to us or from us.

What's an example of a receiver wound?

If we had an angry father, we might always hear God as angry, regardless of tender prophetic content.

Can you give an example of a giver wound?

Consider Jennifer, who has been harmed by Charles, and has developed anger toward men in general. When later prophesying to Nick, she might add into the message extra words that judge him.

That's why Jesus said to clear the major block from your own viewpoint before telling another to remove their minor block. [Matt 7:3]

Being unhealthy in a field we are prophesying about is called "prophesying out of the wound."

This is no small deal. Everyone's childhood hurts loom larger, but I notice because our sensitive prophetic side gets hit when young. Other teachers have commented on this issue too.

Another area to consider might also be the particular relationship between giver and receiver?

Yes. If both are wounded, in opposite ways, there can arise a warped dysfunctional "prophetic codependency."

This situation happens when a prophet has an unhealthy need to exert influence over another; and the other has an unhealthy need to be influenced. That relationship should first be repaired before exchanging anything.

How can we get healing?

Simply inviting God straight into the greatest pain is a first step. The healing process will probably involve forgiveness, repentance, receiving new habits, etc.

In an area where we are wounded, is it better not to deliver a message?

Not true. Always ask the Spirit. Sometimes we're at *more* risk by not speaking. It depends on the size of the wound, the importance of the issue, timing, etc.

To offer an analogy, I know many friends who use mobile phones with smashed glass, rather than upgrade. Sometimes it's most costly to wait, sometimes not. We'll know.

If God is silent, which side to we err on?

You have to know yourself and your environments. Generally, in the U.S. we err on the side of reserved caution.

Regardless, the greater risk is always not hearing true prophecy, rather than hearing false prophecy—because it's Christ's voice that is our best discernment!

In fact, that's the very reason false prophecy exists is divert us from the genuine voice of God.

Since we are always in the process of being healed, we need effective discernment tools.

3.6—DISCERNMENT

These tips are so simple, yet so overlooked.

In the end, discernment isn't that tough to understand, but let's venture into some details, for reminders.

Oh no, more details?

Way to hang in there. If this is too much info overload, then don't worry about finishing. These FAQs can be used as a reference.

Some of the ideas are basic Christianity, scrunched into this subject material.

Is the way to summarize discernment?

Enjoy being God's kid—because who you are determines everything else. So rely more on him than on yourself.

Can you give an example of how this helped you discern a prophecy?

Sure. I have a friend who receives extraordinary, long, intense prophetic words, that intrigue me.

I sent a copy of one of these words to another gifted friend, Zia, who has an off-the-charts ability to detect spiritual presences. She normally liked the messages, but sensed this particular one was inspired by a demon.

At first I was a bit defensive, thinking "But this word is so well-intentioned, so well-written, so scriptural, so challenging."

Later I asked God about it, and the Holy Spirit showed me that the implicit theme of the message was about relying on self-effort. I also had to admit that I had previously ignored the oppressive aura on it too. It was just the type of word that would throw off someone like me, since I sometimes depend way too much on my own abilities. If the dark advice had been any more blatant, I would have caught it.

As a result, I now have my weak walls more fortified and have increased the priority of trusting over trying.

Can we make those discernments without actually seeing the message?

Sometimes. In Zia's case, she more frequently experiences the presences without even reading them.

This "discernment of spirits" gift has proven reliable to many. But it doesn't matter, because anyone can just bring the issue to God and get a triangulation for their own discernment, which is what I did.

Why is discernment so complicated?

The idea is simple—we are complicated. ;)

Isn't it simply all about love?

Yes. But my main point here is to focus on the *center* of love, not the periphery.

For instance, we tend to think Jesus was successful because of his impressive talents, but Jesus let those fade back (mild wealth, average looks, volatile popularity, etc.) and relied on his *core-to-core* heart connection.

God gives the most important part of himself.

Wow, that's so true. Why do we get lost on that?

One reason for that is because our culture tends to promote externals over internals. That's backwards.

Satan assaulted Christ by questioning his identity, twisting Bible passages to accuse him. It's the same today.

Why do we value the exterior over the interior?

Externals appear to be more under our control. and make us feel safer.

But Aquinas (building on Aristotle) said:

"The slenderest knowledge that may be obtained of the highest things is more desirable than the most certain knowledge obtained of lesser things."

So it's just easier to rely on externals.

They are a natural starting point, because that's what we encounter upfront, whether it's a woman's figure or movie's special effects. Those gifts are designed to bring us toward the heart internals, but they might not.

When we fail to move from outside to inside, is to be "objectified," that is, the inner subjective dimension is disregarded, devalued, dishonored. etc. [John 7:24]

So just because a message is clever or accurate or pious doesn't necessarily mean it's from God.

True. We have to go further. For instance, elegant craft by itself doesn't tell the whole story because it might be a *beautifully-worded lie*.

Remember, demons can imitate every part of a prophetic message—except the central love, the exchange of selves, life-giving unity.

Again, a prophetic gift simply helps manifest a spiritual essence.

That's a good philosophy.

In fact, here's a helpful way I like to look at it, using the philosophical language of "matter" and "essence."

Evil can use love's matter (e.g., money, time, imagery, thoughts, emotions, knowledge, doctrines, practices), but not love's essence (God's self-gift).

In other words, a person can give the attributes of love without ever giving themselves. God is not like that. [I Cor 13:2]

So don't judge a message based on particular attributes, but on whether it reveals God's self-gift to you.

Exactly.

That's very comforting.

Well, God loves you from his core.

That's great. But now can we get to some discernment principles that are more down-to-earth?

Do we have to do principles? I don't want to turn this into a self-help book, like "29 Steps to Falling in Love."

But they do help.

All right, but the first principle is to obey what you already know before you seek more knowledge!

C'mon!

I'm not kidding! It's pretty simple. Jesus says "If you obey, you will know." [John 7:17]

There's actually very little in the Bible about discernment! Little kids don't "discern" much. They just hear, obey, and get loved around.

But even kids need to know what to obey.

Just be faithful to the last thing you heard.

"Faith is taking the first step even when you don't see the whole staircase."—Martin Luther King, Jr.

So obeying is more important than hearing?

Obeying completes the message. Hearing is being told to visit the beach, whereas obeying is actually going there.

But that doesn't mean you don't test the words.

Of course, but don't overanalyze either. God always speaks to me more acutely when I obey. ;)

There's got to be more discernment advice than simply hear and obey.

With that reliably firm, let's go into more specifics.

Here's some obvious, well-known principles. These may seem academic, but it's good to keep them in mind for when they are needed. We'll look at a few more interesting insights afterward.

1. Does the message empower love of God and others? Oddly, this is the most important and most neglected.

2. Does the source of the message agree Jesus is God? [I John 4:2]

I have a friend who was a professional psychic (and very accurate), but converted to Christianity because one day she encountered Satan—and had no way to deal with him without Jesus.

Steer clear of anyone who does not acknowledge Jesus, and the reality of the ex-angels who refuse surrender. A psychic can be well-intentioned, yet astonishingly unaware of any dark agent puppeteering them.

3. Does the messages agree with the universal love letter: the Bible? That is, does God's word to you harmonize with God's word to everybody? Does it agree with the church universal, those truly covenanted to God?

4. Is the message self-contradictory? Does a smaller word line up with a bigger word? Does what is less certain support what is more certain? Does the message support previous permanent commitments, such as marriage?

We always seem to forget to consider the context.

Each subplot of our life fits into God's larger plot.

At the influential Bethel church in Redding, California, I heard the insightful illustration (Kris Vallotton) that false prophets build their house on sand—only on tiny parts of the rocks, not the integrated whole. That is, lies have to use random, isolated scriptures but not the integrated, big narratives.

It wasn't too hard to recount these principles.

Well, what we've discussed above are principles that distinguish good from evil. Those are more straightforward. But the trickier ones are discern between two goods.

If the enemy can't tempt us to disobedience outright, he'll next try to knock us off balance into a face plant.

What do you mean "knock us off balance"?

For example, the prophecy should have a healthy mix of hard and soft love, like a good parent gives you.

Watch out if all the messages are about surrendering, but never receiving, or vice versa; or all about consolation, but never correction; or all about the cross, but not about the resurrection.

By "balance" do we mean 50–50?

Not at all. Balance doesn't require symmetry. It depends on the material. For example, not all photos should be 50% bright and 50% dark. Relationships are much more of an art.

Before we wrap up this part on discernment, are there any other important balances to be aware of?

Yes, let's look at one more: God is both outside us and inside us.

Because you're in God's family, he always "mirrors" himself in you. That is, whenever a message's point of view stands only outside you, as if condemning, rather than someone inside helping, then it's probably not from the Holy Spirit who dwells within. [John 14:17]

Centers are always internal. God is so close, we might miss him! He comes disguised as you. Jesus said "the Kingdom of God is within you." [Luke 17:21]

That's good. We need to realize that God is already inside.

And that brings us back to where we started: our identity is in God.

That's a lot to ponder. I think I've had enough thinking.

Good thought.

But I believe I get the main idea. It comes down to just being with God, and he can tell us.

That's it. In the end it's all about enjoying God's love.

We may even feel it's too difficult, but he never wants anything more than your heart, in each present moment. In the future he'll want nothing more either.

For me, the premium encouragement is not even what God says, but simply his presence.

One of the first times that God spoke something clearly to me, I barely remember what he said. The beginning words of the prophecy were "My son…" and the rest I forgot because it was so remarkable to me that God would say that. I'm in his family.

3.7—The Larger Team

Christianity is a team sport.

One benefit from the team is getting more reliable prophetic discernment?

The Bible says we can get independent confirmation (two or three). Since prophecy is designed to build the group, it makes sense to have others refine it.

If nothing is "off," then the church says you are free to believe it, but not obligated. Many magnificent writings in church history fall into this category.

When did you have someone confirm a message?

There have been so many. Really. I've been at prayer meetings where two people saw the same vision and could describe details before the other person could vocalize them. I've experienced prophetic sensations in my body telling me where someone else was feeling pain without knowing it ahead of time. I've had people give me direct specifics about situations they knew nothing about, yet I had the independent details to confirm.

Here's one fun example of a team healing: I had chronic eye pain and received laying on of hands prayer from a friend who said the Lord told her he was going to heal me. I kept praying for months and waiting—yet didn't feel any better. I finally asked a second friend to pray and we asked the Lord what was going on.

Right then God showed her a vision of the devil clamping a vice grip on my eye and an angel next to him holding a blow-torch and saying to me, "If you fast, I'll blast that thing off." So the next day rather than eat meals I took extra dedicated time to worship God.

At the end of the day I went to a third friend and told him of the instruction. He again did the laying on of hands prayer with me and the Lord spoke through him to me saying, "It is indeed My will to heal you. I want you to continue to do the things you love to do for Me."

That's all I needed to hear. We then commanded the enemy off and I felt distinct, instant physical relief. Not only that, within less than a second life felt like springtime again. It was shockingly awesome, like a wonderful oceanic mist in the air. Sometimes we just don't know how much unnecessary suffering we carry until we get release.

When I got home, a fourth friend from my prayer group just happened to send me an e-mail with a graphic of a sad face because there was a vice on its head! The caption was "Did You Ever Have a Day Like This?" And then in the next frame of the cartoon the vice was gone and a beaming smiley face said, "Be grateful—God loves you."

(I thought she must have previously talked with the other friend who had the original vision, but remarkably they had not. I had never seen those images before and haven't since.)

And that's just one story?

Yes. I like that testimony because it shows the combination of worship, several intercessors, fasting, perseverance, and four common charisms experienced: healing, prophecy, tongues, and visions.

Once you experience a few of these, then you notice patterns. To see them clearly, keep a prayer journal or find a spiritual director.

The Bible encourages mentorship.

Directors, mentors, and life coaches, especially ones with credible, holy, supernatural competence are worth the search.

They can provide detached perspectives, pattern recognition, and accountability feedback.

However, their job is less about pointing to right roads, and more about helping avoid the wrong ones.

They are like sound mixers at a concert refining your performance from offstage.

What if I don't believe I need the advice?

Coaches can give advice if you want, but that's unnecessary. Their service is to just hold a mirror, so you can better see how God sees you.

In fact, the most important thing they do is pray for a greater impartation of spiritual power.

Though unpopular today, there's something godly about one good person submitting to another good person, as Jesus does to the Father (or even Luke to Obi-wan). There's a grace in it. Perhaps try it for six months.

What if the relationship becomes toxic?

You'll know if it goes south, such as when authority promotes their opinions as God's will for you on subjective matters, like insisting on who to marry. That's disastrous.

Seriously, watch out for anyone, authority or not, who pushes their will onto your freedom. Whether blatant or subtle, it will always be brutal. It's a form of disguised witchcraft. In fact, in the church this "Christian witchcraft" can occur when one believer imposes what they think God's will is on another on matters of liberty.

How can I protect myself from another pushing their will on me?

There's no substitute for God leading via your conscience. Period. Guard that life.

John Paul II: "The human person is a unique and incommunicable being. He is inviolable, totally unable to allow another person to decide for him. When someone tries to force a choice, the person's free will forms an impassible frontier against the other. The person is, and must be independent, (in Latin, *incommunicabilis*)."

The short answer is don't accept any manipulation, especially supernatural manipulation. Agree with God to block this violation, and command it off.

But what about those who say I can't trust my own conscience because it can be deceived?

Of course, each person's healthy conscience needs to be tightly integrated with the healthy consciences of everyone else, but there is still a priority. Your eyes are the best way to see your world perspective, but everyone else's eyes are indispensable support too. Your heart is the top determiner of whether you're in love; but others can help bring out your heart.

Your conscience is always your highest authority, your greatest connection to God. That's why Paul asks "Why is my freedom being judged by another's conscience?" [I Cor 10:29]

No one has the right to supersede your assigned free will. That is basic to being a person, because without it, our ability to love God is severely hindered.

Regarding prophecy—and this is important—a prophetic word is *only* of value to you insofar as it enhances your own spirit's leading. The prophecy never replaces your conscience.

How does this truth affect the messages in this collection?

As with the rest of life, just talk with God about it.

As terrific as prophetic words can be, we must remember they are spoken to a unique person, at a certain time, with a personality temperament type, in a particular season of life. For you and me, these words are expendable blessings, even when aimed straight at us. The only non-negotiable is responding to the Holy Spirit within, with whatever he asks.

To illustrate, God might instruct a strong person to tackle difficult challenges. But if another person has been traumatized, like a rescue puppy, then words to zealously rally may do more damage. You don't shout at someone on crutches to "score touchdowns!" The heroic thing for them may be just learning how to relax with God.

Since everyone has a unique history with the Lord, then no one prophetic revelation can be treated as a universal principle by itself.

What about severe words of rebuke? How can we tell if they are from God?

One big clue is that a convicting word from God will judge what you did, not who you are.

Here are more indicators. It's the difference between:

the child corrected vs. orphaned/enslaved,
conviction vs. condemnation,
a tree pruned vs. a tree killed.

It's hard to give a word of bad news.

Yes, but the good news about bad news is that God reveals it so we can pray it away! He loves mercy.

"God never gives us discernment in order that we may criticize, but that we may intercede."—Oswald Chambers.

Challenge those who regularly forecast doom as a badge for their own accuracy.

Are there any other keys to giving or receiving a tough word?

Yes. A person only has the right to speak into another's heart to the degree of shared tenderness.

"When you touch the souls of men, you are touching the most precious thing there is. No work is more demanding of wisdom. Seek Me continually for direction and for understanding, so that you may be able to gather the overripe fruit without bruising it." —*Progress of Another Pilgrim* by Frances J. Roberts.

How does timing factor in when delivering a message?

In a group setting, such as a prayer team, there's usually an appointed or implied leader, who helps determine the group's response and application. Hopefully this happens effortlessly without being too mechanical.

But without a designated driver, the vehicle is vulnerable to having multiple people with hands on the steering wheel.

Paul says the spirit of the prophet is under control of the prophet, and thus things should be in order. [I Cor 14:31]   Be open to delivery later or in private.

God knows we'll need to play with it to get it right.

What are tips for delivering messages?

Relate to others as you would prefer to be addressed.

For instance, I've found much involves practicing delicate, considerate language.

What are some language suggestions?

1. One way to intercept possible tension is to re-word the intro from "the Lord is saying…" to "I think the Lord is saying…" That disarms the perception of implied compliance.

2. Declare growth. For instance, saying "God is making you compassionate" can be misinterpreted, so perhaps say instead "God is increasing your compassion."

Since the prayer place is a sacred space we need to be more careful.

According to personality studies, only about 25% of the population is intuitive, big-picture oriented and will understand you even with rough syntax. The other 75% is more detail-oriented and literal, and could accidentally trip on poor wording. We don't need to be paranoid about this, just aware.

3. Use "open-ended language" which leaves room for a person to not feel capped, which is very important when delivering any critique.

In other words, you can never be too encouraging about God's love for someone; but you can be too critical about behavior and then damage a person's core.

So don't negatively label a person's identity.

Even if true, it's dangerous to say, "You are not kind." Again, it's better to say "God is increasing your kindness." Why?

First, because everyone has some amount of kindness; so it's probably more correct.

Second, it might be interpreted as referring to their identity, instead of their quality.

Third, a person may receive a negative word as a curse and turn it into a reality. That is, if you tell a person that they are not kind, then they become less kind because they believe that's who they really are, instead of how God sees them.

By the way, using open-ended language is great practice for all of life, not just prophetic words, because that is reality—God has an infinite upside.

Are you saying we should consider their reaction?

Yes, but we're not responsible for their response. Do your best, then let it go. Even Jesus was sometimes misunderstood. It's O.K..

I'm guessing you'd say it's not that complicated.

I know there's a lot of info here, so take what works and ignore the rest. Whenever it sounds needlessly complex, we always default back to simply love God and others.

In the end there's no coded, impersonal, abstract rule for discernment any more than there can be for love. It's between you and God.

Here's an example: one time God spoke to me via a vision, in which Jesus asked me "Dave, how do you know the difference between what you *think* my will is, and what it really is?"

It's a good question, isn't it?

What's the answer?

He has to tell us!

3.8—Travel Gear for Home

We've covered a lot of material quickly.

Yeah, sorry! Unpack the snacks as needed. And a lot more could be said, but this much will help.

In these last pages, we'll pick up a few more goods for our pilgrimage to eternity.

Like what goods?

Like the most important, super simple ability.

What is that ability?

It turns out our greatest act is unconditional worship—just falling on our faces until we get filled up with God's presence. Heart-to-heart. That's always a direct short cut.

"More is accomplished by spending time in God's presence than by doing anything else."—Heidi Baker

Why didn't you mention this earlier?

Because we need many things, but this is the best.

What do we mean by unconditional worship?

That is where we don't think too much about the mechanics, but just celebrate God with as much of our being as possible.

How much? Jesus says "with all your heart, mind, soul, energy, etc." [Matt 22:37]

When totally submitted, life details have a way of taking care of themselves. Sometimes God's presence will be so palpable in that type of worship that the Spirit arrives like in a flood of favor. Angels distribute healing that doesn't even have to be requested.

Before disbelieving this, we should try it, perhaps periodically for a few weeks. At the very least, survey the places where this is happening and note the effects. There's plenty to see on YouTube alone.

That's great. Worship really changes us?

Some use expressions like being "ruined by God" as an idiom, or some refer to the "Shekinah" glory, referencing the Hebrew experience of the heavenly cloud of God in the temple. God gives us these revelations to help us stay in his presence. That's the main point of gifts.

The effect of holy character imparted by such occurrences is evidence of the transformation.

You like to say that "charisms amplify character." But what if I'm already a nice person?

Congratulations. "Nice" work. ;)

But remember that miracles are to character what a guitar amplifier is to an electric guitar. Our goal is not natural niceness, but supernatural niceness. It's *Christ's* niceness flowing through us.

Besides, wouldn't it be strange if someone wanted to befriend you and you replied "Don't worry, I'm already nice!" Yet amazingly that's how we might respond to God. (He knows we can be weird, but still loves us.)

So charisms are boosters.

They are like fruit fertilizer—literally *miracle grow*. Life enhancers.

Actually, Jesus gave us a specialized prayer to receive these intimacy gifts with God, called the Baptism in the Holy Spirit, which he also described as a baptism of fire.

So there's a baptism of water and a baptism of fire?

Jesus said so in every Gospel. They are like a commitment and a first kiss. (Note that they can happen in either order.)

I guess that's one way to see it.

Here's another, less "sensual" analogy, if preferred:

Water baptism is being saved from drowning via a life jacket, whereas fire baptism is getting equipped to be on the rescue team, throwing life jackets.

You would probably say the personal analogy is better.

Jesus uses both types, but since God is personal, yes, personal is always closer to his heart.

How does one receive this prayer, the Baptism of the Spirit?

Anyone can receive it anywhere, just as in the Gospels.

But the biblical standard avenue was for others who had experienced it to impart this power via the laying on of hands prayer, which is an expression of unity. This is because Holy Spirit is not primarily "taught" but "caught."

Remember that texts like this are mere outer knowledge, while personal experience is inner. It's the difference between reading a book on marriage and being married.

This is how most experience Christ's charisms such as healing, visions, prophecy, and the experience of tongues.

You said before that via the gift of tongues God "prays for you." Is this for real?

That's in the Bible, and is widely prevalent today. It's not always talked about openly—probably because it seems confidential—but like kissing, it can be either public or private.

And that may explain why it's a sensitive subject.

Based on my experience and reported demographics, you probably already know friends currently exercising the gift of tongues, but you might not realize it.

How does the gift of tongues work?

It's similar to receiving prophetic words in that you get "input"—but in this case it's words in your mouth, not words in your ears—that you know didn't originate primarily with you.

I know that sounds unbelievable, so perhaps talk to trusted people who are certain they have it. They can better ascertain the counterfeits. Seek them out, not the unsure, uninformed, unreceptive, or inexperienced.

So how do tongues relate to prophecy?

Peter Kreeft says that in the Bible, and in modern experience, prophecy and tongues are often experienced together because they form a type of interactive dialogue: Tongues is speaking on our behalf to God, whereas prophecy is speaking on God's behalf to us.

There's more to tongues than is first apparent.

The frequency and manner of how we receive prophetic words are heightened while exercising the intimacy of tongues.

For this publication, the signature relevancy of tongues is that it's a flammable catalyst for prophecy.

So people who have tongues tend to experience more prophecy?

That's definitely been my experience in praying with people. These gifts go together.

And what I'm about to say now is something I believe the Lord told me that seems pretty wild. You don't have to believe it, but it explains much.

It may seem a bit too forward for some, so brace yourself: Tongues is a type of contemplative kissing with God, interspersed with loving words. It's a more profound type of "interceding."

I know that may sound too steamy, but when we go back and read the Bible with that renewed view—that God is an adventure romantic—the epic comes alive.

Regardless of how we explain it, tongues is a mysterious, wordless, ineffable exchange, and it becomes most obvious and best known by activating it.

If that's true, then it seems that anyone could experience the gift of tongues?

I wouldn't push this, but here's my opinion:

In the same way everyone gets prophetic words, yet some get it more regularly; so also everyone has the gift of tongues, yet some exercise it more regularly. Neither prophecy or tongues is a requirement, but everyone has them, as free gifts. (This matches the speaking and kissing theme: anyone can engage.)

Based on just Bible texts alone, there's no way to prove or disprove this explanation, but I've honestly never met anyone sincerely hungry who was let down. That's why I make such a big deal about desire. I did have one friend who earnestly sought it, yet didn't receive it until three years later, and that tested my conviction. And I'm not cemented to my speculation, but there definitely seems to be an overall pattern.

In my case, I went for four months of rising levels of hunger, before I finally uncorked the wine and imbibed in the real deal, when the spirit was right. Every relationship's music has different timing.

What if I've already asked for these things?

Then the next activity is very counter-cultural, un-American, unproductive, radical, rare—and may feel a bit like an interior crucifixion: just wait in worship.

In the Bible we have the model for waiting for the Spirit to "arrive" at the Pentecost party, which is something like a prelude, or a romantic anticipation prior to the ecstatic release.

Regardless of what we think happens, God will always reward us.

Must I experience something during worship?

No. But in too many places it's unfortunately more common not to expect much of anything.

We can compare our experience to Jesus. If he's not our standard, what is our standard and why?

For example, when I was younger I used to errantly think that I couldn't ask God for the supernatural revelation, assuming it was as rare as the Bethesda angel in John 5. But one of the introductory lessons God spoke to me through a personal prophetic word was that I can request his voice anytime—because the joy of receiving connects us. [John 16:13]

Wait—I thought these experiences were extraordinary and thus infrequent?

It's extraordinary in quality, but not quantity. Sexuality is extraordinary, but hardly infrequent.

Christ doesn't say "I only relate to you at extraordinary times." God loves communion. No one loves it more.

Personally, I could listen to God all day. He has the coolest vocal.

This is great. But it's a challenge to believe without others.

We need others; they need us. [I Cor 12:26]

In fact, that leads us to our last, crucial point: Get plugged into an environment where the Holy Spirit is genuinely manifesting and not just being talked about. You'll know it by the satisfaction in your own spirit.

Ask God for kindred people. You can't just meet sporadically. Jesus said the seed must "persevere" for the harvest. Investing brings results. [Luke 8:15]

Worship takes time from other things.

Yes, something within is going to have to die for Christ to manifest more life. There's no way around it.

And some of the greatest rewards come after hurdling dangers based on direction from God.

This is important: When God gives a unique promise to us, then we incur a risk *regardless*—by having faith in it or not. Inaction can be a phantasm of security. [Matt 25:25]

When Jesus denied a request, it was only because trust was missing, not religious gymnastics!

Now I'm ready for more. How does one release fear?

Well, what else can be said? Bring it to Christ and ask him what he gives you in its place.

Jesus is the gentle-man who wants to impart his luscious abundance more than we want it.

Love is the greatest. [I Cor 13:8]

That's the key: Love.

When a person marinates into the reality that God loves them, it's absolutely astonishing.

Even the smallest thought of it is staggering. God gave his life for you. We can never come to the end of that. In Heaven we won't either.

So now we're at the end of the book. This has been quite a trip.

Yes. It's ineffable. So let's just enjoy God.

Do you want to lead us in a wrap-up prayer?

"Holy Spirit, have your way!"

Any other final comments?

Thanks for reading! And especially thanks for your prayers. Many abundant blessings to you as well.

If you know someone who might benefit from this, please recommend the book.

I can't answer email, but if we've missed anything important in this first edition (9/1/15), perhaps I'll include more notes for future endeavors at:

http://abundance.davenevins.com

Let's go with the Spirit.

Made in the USA
Middletown, DE
22 November 2017